PEEKING INTO

Computer Science

Customized for CPSC 203
University of Calgary

Second Edition
JALAL KAWASH

Learning Solutions

New York   Boston   San Francisco
London   Toronto   Sydney   Tokyo   Singapore   Madrid
Mexico City   Munich   Paris   Cape Town   Hong Kong   Montreal

Cover Art: Courtesy of brandXpictures.

Pearson Learning Solutions, 501 Boylston Street, Suite 900, Boston, MA 02116
A Pearson Education Company
www.pearsoned.com

Printed in Canada

4 5 6 7 8 9 10 XXXX 15 14 13 12

000200010270587293

MHB

ISBN 10: 0-558-76132-1
ISBN 13: 978-0-558-76132-5

Table of Contents

CHAPTER 1

Problems, Solutions & Computers

Computer science is the discipline that involves studying computers and utilizing them to solve problems. Knowing how to operate a computer does not make a person a computer scientist, just as knowing how to use tools, such as saws and screwdrivers, does not necessarily make someone a carpenter. Carpenters have certain methods and approaches that they follow in order to accomplish tasks. While solving a problem, a carpenter will employ some tools and exclude others. Not only does the carpenter need to know how to operate these tools, he or she needs to know how to use them in the best possible way to solve the problem.

The main goal of computer scientists is solving problems by using computers. Computers are complex and versatile machines; that is why computer scientists are normally very creative. Since the problems computer scientists tackle are to be solved using computers, they have to be able to "think" like a computer. This is not easy! As intelligent creatures, we take many things for granted when we are thinking about a problem or a solution.

With the proliferation of computing devices, most university and college graduates are expected to work with computers. Though they do not need to be computer scientists, they should know how to use computers as tools to solve problems in their own domains. Hence, the methodology used by computer scientists can be useful in other fields. Professionals from other disciplines must think like computer scientists when it comes to using computers to solve their discipline-specific problems.

This chapter defines problems and solutions, as seen by computer scientists. In addition, it introduces two important methods that computer scientists use when thinking about problems and solutions: *divide and conquer* and *abstraction*. Finally, we will look at the internal architecture and components of a modern computer and how information is represented inside the computer.

1

1.1   Problems & Solutions

A problems has *input* and *output*. Making a wooden table is a "problem" whose input is wood, nails, and other material, and its output is a finished wooden table. A cooking "problem" requires the input of ingredients, and its output is cooked food. A *problem* is the specification of the relationship between input and output. A *computational problem* is a problem that can be solved by a computer.

The problem specifies *what* needs to be done. It is not concerned with *how* it is done. The solution to the problem specifies the *how*. The solution is a sequence of instructions that convert the input to the desirable output. In computer science, solutions are called *algorithms*.

Example 1.1 _____

Getting directions

The problem of getting directions can be specified as follows:

Input: Two addresses, address1 and address2

Output: Step by step directions on how to get from address1 to address2

This problem can have several solutions. One popular solution is achieved through using a computer program called Google maps. _____

Example 1.2 _____

Searching the Web

Searching the Web is something that we are accustomed to doing. It is a computational problem that can be specified as follows:

Input: A collection of *keywords*

Output: A ranked list of Web documents that are relevant to the input keywords

The Web documents output can consist of Web sites, images, movies, etc. and are often called *hits*. _____

As end-users, we are often satisfied with the *what*. I input a collection of keywords and I receive a list of relevant documents. Nevertheless, many of us are curious about *how* this is done. That is, how is the Web search problem solved? The solution is achieved through a large program called a *search engine*.

Before the search engine can be used to search for documents, it has to collect and record information about Web documents. Such a collection is called a *database*. A search engine has programs called *Web crawlers* or *spiders* whose job is to collect information about the available documents on the Web and record it in the search engine database. Imagine that you open a Web document and then you systematically open every hyperlink in that page, recording information about every document you encounter. This is what Web crawlers do. They are constantly "searching" the Web and recording information in the search engine database about every Web document they encounter. Such documents are recorded in the database in an indexed way, allowing them to be easily located based on keywords.

Now that the search engine database is populated, you can search it by supplying the keywords through a *Web browser*. These keywords are transformed into a *query*, which is a question submitted to the search engine database. Information about the Web documents that match this search criteria is fetched, ranked according to relevance, and shown to you in the browser.

Computer programs

Solutions to computational problems are represented by *programs*. A program is a sequence of instructions, each telling the computer to do a specific thing. Programs must be written in a language that computers can understand. Such a language is called programming language. An *algorithm* is similar to a program, except that algorithms need not be written in a programming language. A Web crawler algorithm may look like the following:

to-visit = a non-empty list of initial URLs to be visited

For each URL in *to-visit*:

    Open that URL document d

    Record information about d in the database

    Scan d for hyperlinks

    For each hyperlink in d:

        Add the hyperlink to *to-visit*

Web crawlers are *specialized* programs that are designed to solve specific problems. A large class of computer programs can be used as a tool to solve a variety of problems. Such *application* programs include Microsoft Excel.

By the Way — Microsoft Excel Spreadsheets ————————————————

A *spreadsheet* is a grid of *cells* used to organize data into rows and columns. Spreadsheets are important tools that can be used to solve a range of problems that require organizing and analyzing data. There are several computer application programs that create and manage spreadsheets. One such application is Microsoft Excel, which is part of the Microsoft Office suite. The following is a sample spreadsheet:

	A	B	C	D	E	F
1	Invoice Number	124				
2	Date	18/04/2010				
3	Customer	Saleh Dice				
4	US-CAD Rate	1.15				
5						
6	Serial Number	Item Description	Individual Price	Quantity	Total Price	Total CAD Price
7		1 Kindle Wireless Reading Device	$ 256.00	2	$ 512.00	CAD 588.80
8		2 Avatar (Two-Disc Blu-ray/DVD Combo)	$ 24.99	3	$ 74.97	CAD 86.22
9		3 Wines of Central & Southern Italy	$ 8.98	2	$ 17.96	CAD 20.65
10						
11	Invoice Total				$ 604.93	CAD 695.67

The columns in a Microsoft Excel spreadsheet are referred to by letters: A, B, C, etc. The rows are referred to by numbers. The cell where a column and a row intersect is refereed to by the combination of the column and row references. For instance, the top-right cell (containing **Invoice Number**) in the spreadsheet is cell A1, the invoice number **124** is in cell B1, and the invoice total of **$ 604.93** is in cell E11.

An important feature of Microsoft Excel is the ability to perform calculations. The field **Total Price** is calculated as **Individual Price × Quantity**. To perform calculations in Microsoft Excel, the cell contents must start with an equal sign =. This is called a *formula* and it instructs Excel to perform a calculation. In cell E7, the formula is **=C7*D7**; that is, the contents of cell E7 is the result of the multiplication (computer programs use * for ×) of the values in cells C7 and D7. The value of a formula is automatically re-calculated each time the values of the cells referenced in the formula change. For instance, if you change the quantity of in cell D7 to 3, instead of 2, the value in cell E7 is automatically updated to **$ 768.00**, which is **256*3**.

When copying a cell, by dragging it or copying and pasting it, Excel automatically updates the referenced cells. For instance, if the formula in cell E7 (**=C7*D7**) is copied to cell E8, the copied formula in E8 becomes **=C8*D8**. Copying the formula across rows, changes the row numbers. Similarly, copying the formula across columns change the column references. If the same formula in cell E7 is copied to cell F7, it becomes **=D7*E7**.

The cell references that we have been referring to, such as E7 and C7, are called *relative* references. The cells with relative references are treated relative to their position. For instance, the formula in cell E7, **=C7*D7**, is understood by Excel as the multiplication of the value two columns to the left with the value one column to the left. Hence, when this formula is copied to cell E8, this interpretation is maintained: the value should be the multiplication the cells two and one columns to the left of E8, or **=C8*D8**.

Often, it is desirable to *fix* the reference of a cell while it is copied. Consider the field **Total CAD Price**, where totals are required in both US and CAD currencies. The formula in cell F7 is **=E7*B4**. That is, the CAD equivalent to the US total is the *US-CAD exchange rate* × *the US total price*. If this cell is copied to cell F8, it becomes **=E8*B5**. However, B5 is empty. It gets worse if we copy it to F9, since B6 contains text which cannot be used with multiplication. Therefore, we need to fix the reference to B4 in the formula. This is called *absolute* referencing.

To make a reference absolute in Excel, the column or row reference is prefixed by a dollar sign **$**. The formula in cell F7 should be **=E7*B$4**, instructing Excel to fix the 4; so that when it is copied to F8, it becomes **=E8*B$4**. Note that if for some reason, we decide to copy this formula from F7 to G7, it becomes **=F7*C$4**. The column reference B is not fixed. To make it an absolute column reference, the B must be preceded by **$** (**=E8*$B$4**). Depending on the context, you can fix the column reference, the row reference, or both.

The total formula in cell E11 can be written as **=E7+E8+E9**; however, this becomes cumbersome when adding a large number of cells. Microsoft Excel provides *functions* for easier group calculations. In fact, the formula in cell E11 is **=SUM(E7:E9)**. The colon **:** is used to designated a range of cells. The formula **=SUM(E7:E9)** reads "sum the values from cell E7 to E9". This way, a larger range of cells can be summed in a an easy way, such as **=SUM(H7:H119)**. Functions like SUM allow you to use commas to separate cells, but the meaning of the function will be different. For instance, **=SUM(E7,E9)** sums cells E7 and E9 only.

There are many functions that can be used in Excel. To learn about these, click the *insert function* button:

The insert function window will pop up:

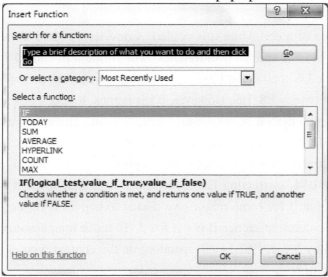

If you type in a description of the required calculation, Excel will give you suggestions for functions.

Visualization of data is a very powerful tool in spreadsheets. Such visual representation in Microsoft Excel is called a *chart*. The following spreadsheet summarizes Canada's performance in the Winter Olympic games since 1924:

	A	B	C	D	E
1	Games	Bronze	Silver	Gold	Total
2	1924 Chamonix	1	0	0	1
3	1928 St. Moritz	1	0	0	1
4	1932 Lake Placid	1	1	5	7
5	1936 Garmisch-Partenkirchen	0	1	0	1
6	1948 St. Moritz	2	0	1	3
7	1952 Oslo	1	0	1	2
8	1956 Cortina d'Ampezzo	0	1	2	3
9	1960 Squaw Valley	2	1	1	4
10	1964 Innsbruck	1	0	2	3
11	1968 Grenoble	1	1	1	3
12	1972 Sapporo	0	1	0	1
13	1976 Innsbruck	1	1	1	3
14	1980 Lake Placid	0	1	1	2
15	1984 Sarajevo	2	1	1	4
16	1988 Calgary (host)	0	2	3	5
17	1992 Albertville	2	3	2	7
18	1994 Lillehammer	3	6	4	13
19	1998 Nagano	6	5	4	15
20	2002 Salt Lake City	7	3	7	17
21	2006 Turin	7	10	7	24
22	2010 Vancouver (host)	14	7	5	26
23	Total	52	45	48	145
24					

To analyze the trend of Canada's performance throughout the history of the games, a line chart can be very informative. Highlight the data that is needed for the chart. From the insert ribbon, choose a line chart:

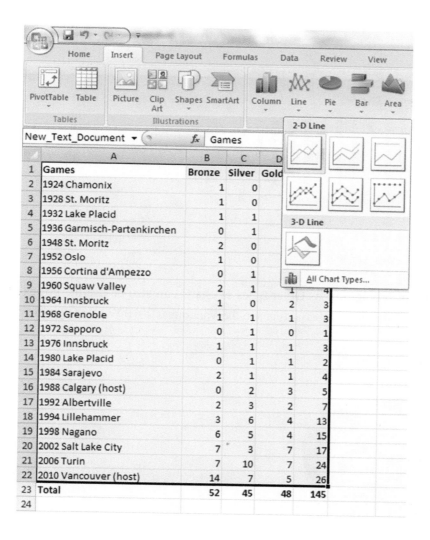

Choosing the first type of a line chart, yields the following chart, which clearly shows a substantial and consistent improvement in the total number of medals since 1988, though there is a dip in the number of gold medals in 2010:

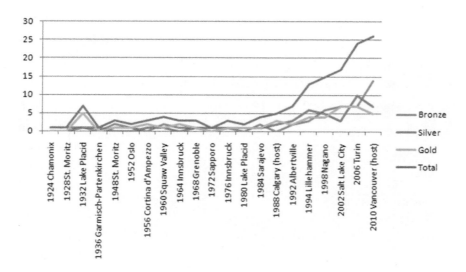

A line chart is appropriate for seeing trends. Other types of charts can also be useful. For example, a pie chart can show the break down of medal types in the Vancouver 2010 Winter Olympics:

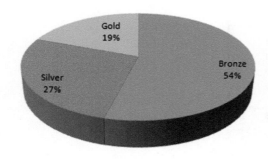

1.2 Divide & Conquer

A solution to a problem, no matter how small, can become overwhelmingly complex. Two important methods that allow us to defuse this complexity are *divide and conquer* and *abstraction*. Abstraction will be discussed in the next section.

Historically, divide and conquer is a policy used by superpowers to keep their subjects divided, allowing superpowers to rule their subjects. This is not exactly how the technique is used in our context. As a problem-solving approach, divide and conquer requires the breaking down of a problem to sub-problems and finding solutions (or sub-solutions) to these sub-problems. The approach can be further applied to the sub-problems, dividing them in turn. Once we have a sub-problem that is easy to solve, no further division is required. The sub-solutions are finally combined together producing a solution to the original problem. Hence, divide and conquer is comprised of three steps: *divide*, *solve*, and *combine*.

Divide and conquer is not limited to computational problems. For instance, carpenters can make use of it. The problem of making a wooden table can be divide into two sub-problems: (1) making the table top and (2) making the legs. These sub-problems are easier to solve than the original problem. Once these components are developed, the last step would be to combine them. Building contractors use divide and conquer as well. To build a house, a contractor delegates various jobs to other trade workers. The contractor hires a framer, plumber, electrician, painter, etc. Doing so, the contractor, divides a complex task into smaller, easier tasks. The framer can also divide the framing job and delegate it to specialized trade workers.

Next, MS Excel and Web search engines will be used as tools to solve a sample problem, which will be tackled using the divide and conquer approach.

Rita is considering moving to one of 15 US states. Her criteria are that the state:

1. has a warm climate,

2. has a low crime rate, and

3. is close to Ottawa.

Rita embarks on solving each of the sub-problems separately:

1. Collect the average high temperature for each state under consideration.

2. Collect homicide rates from these states.

3. Measure the time it takes to drive from each state to/from Ottawa.

Collecting average high temperatures

Doing a Web search for average high temperature for US states, using Google, Rita comes across the URL www.netstate.com:

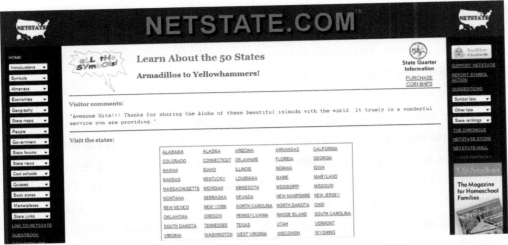

where she finds an enormous amount of information about all US states. In particular, she finds the average high temperature for each state. However, she notices that these temperatures are in Fahrenheit, which she is not comfortable with. She decides to convert these temperatures to Celsius. Rita uses Google as a calculator:

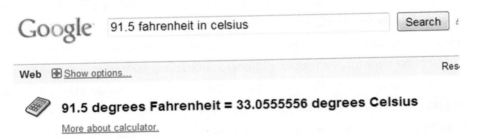

Recording her observations in a spreadsheet for the 15 states under consideration, she gets:

	A	B
1	State	Avg high temperature
2	Alabama	33
3	California	33.44
4	Connecticut	29.33
5	Georgia	33.44
6	Ilinois	30.6
7	Kansas	33.8
8	Louisiana	34
9	Maine	26
10	Maryland	30.6
11	Minnesota	28.55
12	Mississippi	33.6
13	Nebraska	31.94
14	New Hampshire	28.11
15	New York	29.61
16	South Dakota	30.27
17		

This concludes Rita's sub-solution for the first sub-problem.

Collecting homicide rates

While Rita was reading Howard Wainer's *Graphic Discovery: A Trout in the Milk and Other Visual Adventures*, she came across homicide statistics in the US. She decides to use these rates. Updating her spreadsheet, yields:

	A	B	C
1	State	Avg high temperature	HomicideRate
2	Alabama	33	12
3	California	33.44	8.8
4	Connecticut	29.33	3.9
5	Georgia	33.44	8.7
6	Ilinois	30.6	9.8
7	Kansas	33.8	6.1
8	Louisiana	34	16.1
9	Maine	26	1.8
10	Maryland	30.6	10.9
11	Minnesota	28.55	2.8
12	Mississippi	33.6	14.2
13	Nebraska	31.94	3.9
14	New Hampshire	28.11	2.2
15	New York	29.61	6.3
16	South Dakota	30.27	3
17			

Rita is now done with this sub-problem.

Measuring driving time to/from Ottawa

Rita notices that this sub-problem needs to be further divided. Since Rita is not sure where in a potential state she would be living, she has to determine a point in the state so that the driving time can be measured to that point. Hence, this sub-problem is further divided into two sub-problems:

1. Determine a location in the state, and

2. Measure the driving time from/to Ottawa to that location.

Rita can use the geographic center, the capital city, or the point of entry to that state as a point of reference. She decides that the easiest thing would be to choose the capital city. Therefore, she needs to determine the capital city of each of the 15 states. Using Google, she finds the URL www.usacitiesonline.com, which lists all states and their capital cities, side-by-side. This, she thinks, is easier than using www.netstate.com, where she has to navigate to each state page to determine the capital city. Rita decides to record this information on the side, not in her spreadsheet, since she is only using this information temporarily to derive more information.

For measuring the driving time to/from Ottawa, Rita decides to use Google maps:

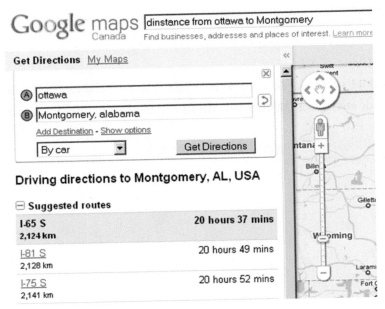

Collecting and recording the estimated driving time to/from Ottawa in her spreadsheet, results in:

	A	B	C	D
1	State	Avg high temperature	HomicideRate	Time to Ottawa
2	Alabama	33	12	20.37
3	California	33.44	8.8	41
4	Connecticut	29.33	3.9	7.12
5	Georgia	33.44	8.7	18.26
6	Ilinois	30.6	9.8	15.19
7	Kansas	33.8	6.1	21.7
8	Louisiana	34	16.1	25
9	Maine	26	1.8	17.13
10	Maryland	30.6	10.9	9.13
11	Minnesota	28.55	2.8	19.7
12	Mississippi	33.6	14.2	22.27
13	Nebraska	31.94	3.9	20.11
14	New Hampshire	28.11	2.2	6.13
15	New York	29.61	6.3	5.25
16	South Dakota	30.27	3	25
17				

The combine step

Now that Rita has solved all the sub-problems separately, she hopes that this will help her solve the original problem. However, she notices that this is not as easy at it seems. Her collected data indicates that her criteria can be conflicting. It looks like that a warmer climate comes with a higher homicide rate. For instance, Louisiana has the highest average high temperature of 34^oC, but also has the highest homicide rate among all 15 states, at 16.1%. She also notices that the closer a states is to Ottawa, the colder it is.

Rita would like to combine all these measures into a single value that allows her to decide on her future home. Since these measure are conflicting, she realizes that she has to prioritize her criteria. Re-thinking her criteria, she discovers that the homicide rate is the most important for her, followed by the warm climate. She comes up with the following weights, which reflect the relative importance of her preferences: 50% for the homicide rate, 30% for temperature, and 20% for the distance to Ottawa. She calculates a weighted average, called *objective value*, for each state, based on the weights she devised. Rita comes up with the following formula:

$$((100 \text{ - homicide rate}) \times 50\%) + (\text{temperature} \times 30\%) - (\text{driving time} \times 20\%)$$

The states with the highest objective values are the ones that Rita should be considering. To favor the states with lower crime rate, she used $(100 \text{ - homicide rate}) \times 50\%$, calculating the "non-crime" rate, so to speak. The higher the homicide rate, the lower $(100 \text{ - homicide rate})$ will be. She added the temperature to the objective value, favoring the warmer states. She also subtracted the driving time from the objective value, favoring the states that are closer to Ottawa. Her final spreadsheet looks like:

	A	B	C	D	E
1	State	Avg high temperature	HomicideRate	Time to Ottawa	Objective Value
2	Alabama	33	12	20.37	49.826
3	California	33.44	8.8	41	47.432
4	Connecticut	29.33	3.9	7.12	55.425
5	Georgia	33.44	8.7	18.26	52.03
6	Ilinois	30.6	9.8	15.19	51.242
7	Kansas	33.8	6.1	21.7	52.75
8	Louisiana	34	16.1	25	47.15
9	Maine	26	1.8	17.13	53.474
10	Maryland	30.6	10.9	9.13	51.904
11	Minnesota	28.55	2.8	19.7	53.225
12	Mississippi	33.6	14.2	22.27	48.526
13	Nebraska	31.94	3.9	20.11	53.61
14	New Hampshire	28.11	2.2	6.13	56.107
15	New York	29.61	6.3	5.25	54.683
16	South Dakota	30.27	3	25	52.581
17					
18					
19	Weights				
20	Temperature	30%			
21	Homicide	50%			
22	Time to Ottawa	20%			

Based on this analysis, Rita narrows her choice down to three states: New Hampshire, Connecticut, and New York, which have the largest objective values:

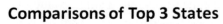

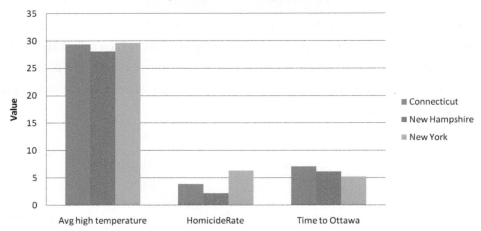

By the Way — Spreadsheet Design

Spreadsheets must be designed so that they are easy to use and modify. A spreadsheet should be a long-lasting device that can be useful to other people, where applicable. No matter how simple you think a spreadsheet is, it may not be readable to other people. Furthermore, it can be hard for you to remember certain details, such as complex calculations, when you come back to a spreadsheet after a long while.

We will outline how to make a spreadsheet long-lasting and useful to others. A spreadsheet should be divided into five sections, each of which can be included in a separate sheet tab. These are: introduction, data, model, data dictionary, and conclusions.

Introduction

A spreadsheet should have a formal introduction that (1) states the purpose of the spreadsheet, (2) provides instructions on how to use it, (3) cites resources, and (4) maps the contents. The introduction section should also have an informative title. For instance, a suitable introduction for Rita's "US states" spreadsheet might be:

	A	B	C	D	E	F	G	H	I	J	K	L	M
1							Which US state should I live in?						
2							Rita Peeking						
3													
4	Overview												September-25-09
5	This spreadsheet was created to aid in deciding which US state we will be moving to. There are three main factors that shall affect our decision.												
6	The US state must:												
7	1. Have a warm climate.												
8	2. Have a low crime rate.												
9	3. Be close to Ottawa.												
10													
11	Data collection												
12	The data for the aforementioned three criteria was collected as follows:												
13													
14	The average high temperatures for each state are obtained from netstate.com[1].												
15	The fahrenheit values are then converted to Celsius using Google calculator[2].												
16													
17	Homicide rates were collected from Wainer's "Graphic Discovery"[3].												
18													
19	The distance to Ottawa was found by using Google Maps[4] to get the distance from the state capital to Ottawa.												
20													
21	Table of Contents												
22	Data:			Contains the raw data and calculations.									
23	Model:			Explains the calculations conducted in the Data tab, as well as listing all formulas used.									
24	Data Dictionary			Explains each set of data so that its type and description are given.									
25	Dashboard:			Contains charts based on the Data tab.									
26													
27	References												
28	1. Nstate LLC. (2009, September 24). Retrieved September 25, 2009, from netstate.com: www.netstate.com												
29	2. Google. (2009, September 25). Google Calculator. Retrieved September 25, 2009, from google.com: www.google.com												
30	3. Wainer, H. (2004). Graphic Discovery: A Trout in the Milk and Other Visual Adventures. Princeton: Princeton University Press.												
31	4. Google. (2009, September 25). Google Maps. Retrieved September 25, 2009, from http://maps.google.com												
32													
33													
34													
35													
36													

Introduction / Data / Model / DataDictionary / Dashboard

Data

This section contains the raw and calculated data. It is the "actual" spreadsheet. Rita's spreadsheet data section is what was developed in the previous section:

	A	B	C	D	E
1	State	Avg high temperature	HomicideRate	Time to Ottawa	Objective Value
2	Alabama	33	12	20.37	49.826
3	California	33.44	8.8	41	47.432
4	Connecticut	29.33	3.9	7.12	55.425
5	Georgia	33.44	8.7	18.26	52.03
6	Ilinois	30.6	9.8	15.19	51.242
7	Kansas	33.8	6.1	21.7	52.75
8	Louisiana	34	16.1	25	47.15
9	Maine	26	1.8	17.13	53.474
10	Maryland	30.6	10.9	9.13	51.904
11	Minnesota	28.55	2.8	19.7	53.225
12	Mississippi	33.6	14.2	22.27	48.526
13	Nebraska	31.94	3.9	20.11	53.61
14	New Hampshire	28.11	2.2	6.13	56.107
15	New York	29.61	6.3	5.25	54.683
16	South Dakota	30.27	3	25	52.581
17					
18					
19	Weights				
20	Temperature	30%			
21	Homicide	50%			
22	Time to Ottawa	20%			

Model

The model section includes the assumptions and calculations. The model should explain three items: (1) data values, (2) tricky formulas, and (3) a complete listing of all formulas used in the spreadsheet. Rita's spreadsheet model can be:

	A	B	C	D	E	F	G	H	I	J	K	L	M	N
1								Model						
2														
3	There are three factors adding to my final preference: The average high temperature, the homicide rate, and the time to Ottawa.													
4	However, the three factors are not of the same importance. Thus, each of the factors is given a *weight* based on how important I think it is.													
5														
6	The weights were decided as follows:													
7	AvgTempWeight		30%											
8	HomicideRate		50%											
9	Time to Ottawa		20%											
10														
11	Since lower homicide rates are clearly preferred, the weight is applied to 100 - HomicideRate.													
12	Also, since a smaller time to Ottawa is preferred, the Time to Ottawa needs to have a negative effect on the final objective value.													
13	Thus, a longer trip time to Ottawa will lead to a lower Objective Value													
14														
15	Hence, the final formula for the Objective Value is:													
16	**Formula for Objective Value**			AvgTemp*AvgTempWeight + (100 - HomicideRate) * HomicideWeight - TimeToOttawa*TimeOttawaWeight										

Data dictionary

For an outsider, it can be hard to understand the meaning of data columns in a spreadsheet. For instance, **Time to Ottawa** can refer to driving, flying, or something else. The purpose of a data dictionary is to explain the meaning of all data fields in a spreadsheet. Each fields should be given a (1) type (such as categorization, raw data, column calculation, or row calculation), (2) data type (such as number, text, percentage, date, time, etc.), (3) reference to the sheet and cells where the data resides, and (4) brief description or narrative of the data. Rita's spreadsheet data dictionary is:

	A	B	C	D	E	F	G
1						Data Dictionary	
2			·				
3							
4	Name	Field Type	Data Type	Sheet/Cell Reference			
5	State	Categorization	Text	Data!A2:A16			
6	Avg high temperature	Raw	Float	Data!B2:B16			
7	Homicide Rate	Raw	Float	Data!C2:C16			
8	Time to Ottawa	Raw	Float	Data!D2:D16			
9	Objective Value	Row Calculation	Float	Data!E2:E16			
10	Weights	Raw	Percentage	Data!B20:B22			
11							

Conclusions

The conclusion section includes summary charts, analysis, and concluding remarks.

1.3 Abstraction

Abstraction is another important method that can help us defuse the complexity of problems and their solutions. Abstraction is the ability to think of a problem at different levels, magnifying the relevant details and hiding the irrelevant ones at each level. Computer scientists have the ability to abstractly define problems and their solutions. They know how and when to isolate and hide some irrelevant details and what other details need to be magnified. To think about problems abstractly, computer scientists use mathematical structures to model these problems and their solutions, such as graphs and trees, which will be studied later in this book.

Abstraction is illustrated through an example. Several wall-hugging robot (or mouse) kits are being sold nowadays. This robot is a complex machine. It has a built-in computer that follows instructions programmed into it. It also has some sensors that allow it to receive signals from the external world. Finally, it has mechanical components that allow it to move around.

The robot we have can perform the following simple operations:

- Move one step forward; all steps are of the same distance

- Make a 90 degree left rotation, staying in position

- Make a 90 degree right rotation, staying in position

The robot has two obstacle sensors mounted on it; one senses forward and another senses to the right. The sensors' range is very small, slightly smaller than the distance covered by the robot in a single forward step.

Our job is to program the robot so that it finds a wall or any other obstacle in a closed area, such as an apartment. Once it finds the wall, it "hugs" it, keeping the wall or obstacle on its right, indefinitely making forward steps, until it is turned off. Hence, when it gets to a corner, the robot has to decide how to turn so that it keeps moving forward, keeping the wall on its right.

This problem is formulated as follows:

Input: objects sensed by the *front sensor* (FS) and the *right sensor* (RS).

Output: movement actions taken by the robot such that it finds the wall, positions the wall on its right, and moves while hugging the wall. The movement actions are: move one step *forward* (indicated by F), rotate *left* (indicated by L), and rotate *right* (indicated by R).

The robot's world

To divide and conquer, we answer two separate questions. The first question that we need to think about is how to model the robot's external world. Since our robot only moves one step at a time and the steps are the same size, it is sufficient to model its world as a grid of equal-sized squares. A square has one of two values: blocked (wall) or free (space). An example layout is given in Figure 1.1, where × indicates obstacles. The size of the squares in the gird is determined by the size of the robot's step.

×	×	×	×	×	×	×	×	×	×
×				×		×			×
×				×		×			×
×			×	×		×			×
×				×		×			×
×				×					×
×									×
×	×	×	×	×	×	×	×	×	×

Figure 1.1: The robot's world as a grid of wall (×) and space squares

We have reduced the robot's world into one of two things: a free square or a blocked square. A bookshelf, a wall, and a couch are all irrelevant details. All that is required here is to regard them as obstacles. This way, the robot's movement takes it from the square it is currently in to the one directly ahead. The sensors can only sense the squares immediately to the front or right of the current robot's position. This approach of reducing the robot's world into one of two things is an example of *abstraction*.

The robot

The second question is modeling the robot itself, which is a complex machine. Yet, for the problem that we are trying to solve, it is sufficient to think of the robot as a black-box, depicted in Figure 1.2.

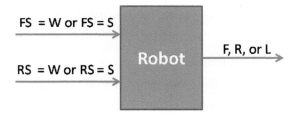

Figure 1.2: The robot as a black-box

The robot accepts two inputs from its external world through its front sensor FS and the right sensor RS. The value sensed is either W for a wall or S for free space. The output of the robot is one of its three possible actions: move **F**orward, rotate **R**ight, or rotate **L**eft. Any other detail about the robot is irrelevant to our purpose and is hidden inside the black-box.

The algorithm

Now that we have all the models in place, exposing the needed details and hiding the unnecessary ones, the remaining task is to *program* the robot so that it hugs the wall. That is, we need to give the robot instructions so that it accomplishes the required task, hugging the wall. Such a program is first represented as an algorithm.

To divide and conquer, we distinguish between two modes: *looking-for-the-wall* and *hugging-the-wall*. When the robot is turned on, it can be anywhere in the robot's world, and it must first find a wall.

Looking-for-the-wall: In the *looking-for-the-wall* mode, the robot will be programmed to keep on moving forward, until it finds the wall, using RS or FS. If RS senses a wall (denoted RS = W), the wall is found, ending the *looking-for-the-wall* mode. If, however, FS senses a wall (denoted FS = W), the robot must rotate left, positioning the wall to its right and ending the *looking-for-the-wall* mode.

Hugging-the-wall: The *hugging-the-wall* mode is more complex than it may appear, so we will divide it to conquer. If the sensors have the values RS = W and FS = S, then the robot moves forward (Figure 1.3(a)).

However, while hugging the wall (RS = W), the robot can reach an inner corner, where FS = W (Figure 1.3(b)). Whenever FS = W, the robot must rotate left, which may restore the original conditions for hugging the wall (RS = W and FS = S). Note that this even works if a single left turn does not restore the condition FS = S. This can take place when the robot enters a dead end (Figure 1.3(c)). Since FS = W, the robot must make a left rotation (Figure 1.3(d)). After the first left rotation, it is still the case that FS = W. Hence, another left rotation is needed to restore the condition (S = S and RS = W. Even if the robot was turned on in a trap square, it will keep on rotating left in its place, and indeed hugging the wall (Figure 1.3(e)).

So far, we have established two rules for the robot while in the *hugging-the-wall* mode:

1. If RS = W and FS = S, then take one step forward

2. If FS = W, then make one left rotation

There is an additional case when the robot gets to an outer corner (Figure 1.3(f)). Since RS = W and FS = S, the robot will move forward (Figure 1.3(g)). This will make RS = S and FS = S. The robot should not move forward any more, since it will lose the wall. Instead, what is required is a right rotation (Figure 1.3(h)) followed by a forward step. This creates the third rule for the robot while in the *hugging-the-wall* mode:

3. If RS = S and FS = S, then

    (a) make one right rotation

    (b) take one step forward

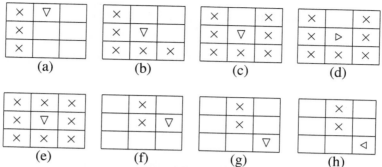

(a) The robot is in *hugging-the-wall* mode. (b) The robot reaches an inner-corner; a left rotation is sufficient. (c) The robot reaches a dead-end. (d) One right rotation in a dead-end; a second right rotation is sufficient to continue motion in the *hugging-the-wall* mode. (e) The robot in a trapped square keeps rotating indefinitely, staying in the *hugging-the-wall* mode. (f) The robot approaches an outer-corner. (g) The robot realizes that it has encountered an outer corner. (h) The robot adjusts direction by rotating right; this is sufficient to keep the robot *hugging-the-wall*.

Figure 1.3: The options of the robot (indicated as △).

Now, we are ready to summarize the robot's algorithm:

***Looking-for-the-wall* mode:** Repeat the following steps:

1. If RS = W, then end the *looking-for-the-wall* mode and go to the *hugging-the-wall* mode

2. If FS = W, then rotate left and end the *looking-for-the-wall* mode and go to the *hugging-the-wall* mode

3. Otherwise, take one step forward (F)

***Hugging-the-wall* mode:** Repeat the following steps:

1. If RS = W and FS = S, then take one step forward (F)

2. If FS = W, then make one left rotation (L)

3. If RS = S and FS = S, then

   (a) make one right rotation (R)

   (b) take one step forward (F)

The implementation

Once an algorithm is found, the next step is to translate it to a program that the robot's computer understands. This implementation of the algorithm requires familiarity with a *programming language* through which the instructions of the algorithm are encoded for the robot's computer to understand and execute.

The implementation takes an abstract algorithm and concretizes it on a physical computer. This requires some understanding of how computers are inside the black-box. Instead of the robot's specialized computer, we will turn our attention to the general-purpose computers that are used in our daily lives.

1.4   Computers

Computers different from other machines because of their versatility. They can be programmed to do many things: play music and movies, send and receive email and instant messages, organize financial records, or control a nuclear plant. Different computers can be built differently, but they all share similar basic structure and functionality.

A computer (Figure 1.4) consists of a *Central Processing Unit* (CPU), *main memory*, *secondary storage*, and *peripheral (I/O) devices*.

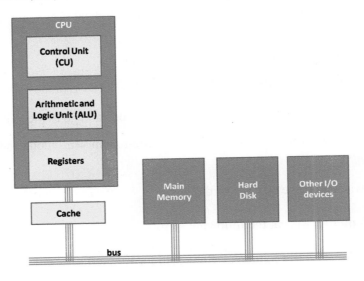

Figure 1.4: Organization of a computer

Buses

All of the computer components are connected by *buses*. A bus is a bundle of thin wires, each capable of carrying one signal, representing a **0** or a **1**. In fact, everything inside the computer must be represented by zeros and ones. It is much easier to build computers this way. **0** can be represented by a low voltage, like an off lamp, and **1** can be represented by a high voltage, like an on lamp. A *binary digit* (abbreviated *bit*) is a single **0** or **1** value. A typical computer has two main buses, an *address* bus and a *data* bus. These buses allow the CPU to interact with other components, such as main memory. As the names suggest, the address bus is used to specify an address in main memory from which or to which data will be read or written, and the data bus is used to transport the read or written data. A typical address bus includes 32 or 64 wires, resulting in what is called 32-bit or 64-bit architectures. A 64-bit data bus can transport data and instructions faster than a 32-bit data bus. For instance, writing a 64-bit word in memory can be done in one shot with a 64-bit bus. However, with a 32-bit bus, this needs to be done in two steps, transferring 32 bits in each step. Hence, the bus width is a factor that affects the machine's overall performance.

CPU

The CPU, also called the *processor*, is the brain of the computer. The CPU executes a program by following its coded instructions. The programs are first stored in secondary storage, such as a hard disk or a CD-ROM. When the program is "opened", it is loaded to the main memory. Once in the main memory, the CPU brings instructions from the main memory and executes them. Any data that the program needs must be also stored in the computer. Such data is stored as *files* in secondary storage and must be loaded to the main memory when needed by the executing program.

The CPU consists of two major sub-components: the *Arithmetic and Logic Unit* (ALU) and the *Control Unit* (CU). The ALU performs simple arithmetic and logic operations, such as adding two numbers. The CU controls the operation of the ALU and other components in the machine. While a CPU is executing a program, it needs a scratch pad memory to store program instructions, data, and intermediate results. Such a scratch pad is provided as a set of *registers*. Each register can hold a program instruction or a data value, such as a number. A register can hold few bits; the actual size may differ from one machine to another. Nowadays, the register size is typically 32 or 64 bits. The number of registers is usually about one to a few dozen, but the actual number may vary from one machine to another.

Main storage

Anything that the CPU operates on must be in the main memory. Main memory is typically referred to by RAM, *Random Access Memory*, for historical reasons. Early computers used tapes (just like outdated music cassettes) for main memory. Tapes are *sequential access memory*; to listen to the last song on the cassette, you would needed to fast forward to the appropriate position progressing through the tape sequentially. There was no way to jump directly to the needed place on the tape, but this is possible with RAM.

Secondary storage

Main memory is *volatile*; it cannot hold any data without a flowing electric current. That is, if you switch off a computer, all that was stored in RAM will be lost. Hence, computers need a non-volatile storage, one that holds data in the absence of electric power. There are different non-volatile or permanent storage devices. These include *hard disks* and *optical disks.*

A hard disk makes use of electro-magnetic signals that stay on a medium in the absence of power. Optical disks, such as CDs and DVDs, burn holes into a thin metal layer that can be read by laser beams. We will have a closer look at both types of these devices later in this section.

Peripheral devices

Computers can have many Input/Output (I/O) devices connected to them. A keyboard and mouse are examples of input devices. Monitors and printers are examples of output devices.

Cache memory

Main memories are fast, but are slower than CPUs, so they typically slow down the CPU's operation. This is why modern machines also include *cache memory* (*cache* is French for hidden). The cache is faster but is much smaller than main memory. A useful analogy here is cooking supplies. If you run out of supplies in the kitchen (the CPU), it would be very costly (time-wise) to run to the supermarket (the main memory) every time you require something. Instead, we typically "cache" some supplies in a pantry (the cache). Of course, the cache can become obsolete (empty, in the kitchen supplies analogy) and occasionally you will need to refurbish it from main memory. Figure 1.4 shows cache memory as part of the computer organization. The cache size is another factor that affects machine performance. A larger cache can improve the overall system performance.

ALU operation

There are only a handful operations that an ALU can perform, such as adding two numbers and negating a value. Any other operation, such as multiplication and subtraction, can be performed from these basic ones. For instance, to multiply 5 and 6, the ALU can add 6 to itself 5 times. To subtract 5 from 6, the ALU can negate 5 and add 6 to negative 5. Similarly, division can be performed using successive subtractions.

The operation of the ALU is explained in Figure 1.5. To perform a basic operation, say adding two numbers, the following steps must be followed:

1. Load the first number from main memory to register A

2. Load the second number from main memory to register B

3. Load the first input register of the ALU from A

4. Load the second input register of the ALU from B

5. Perform an *add* operation

6. Collect the output in the ALU output register (also called the *accumulator*)

7. Load the result back to register C

8. Store register C in main memory

Each of these steps is called a *microinstruction*. A typical computer can perform 2 to 3 billion microinstructions per second. This speed of CPUs is measured in Hertz and is typically called the *clock speed*. A CPU that can perform 2 billion microinstructions per second has a speed of 2 Giga Hertz (GHz). The CPU clock speed is another factor that affects the overall system performance.

CPUs have been consistently made faster over the past decades. This was mainly accomplished by jamming more basic electronic elements, called transistors, into the CPU chip. Now a days, it is normal to combine a billion or more transistors into a chip that is smaller than the size of a credit card. This can result in an overheating problem. With so many transistors located in a very small area, the chip can overheat and this can lead to malfunctioning.

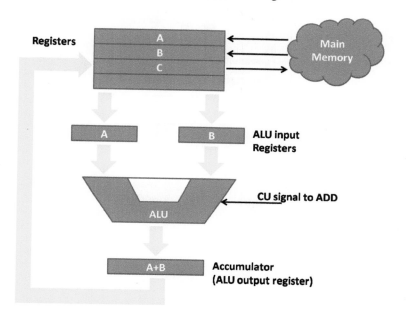

Figure 1.5: Illustrating an ALU ADD operation

Dual-core computers

Processor designers resorted to an old alternative idea to make the CPUs faster. If you're building a brick wall, you may hire one mason to do the job. Imagine that this is the fastest mason on earth, and it takes him or her 30 days to finish the wall. Can we build the wall in a shorter period of time? We can if we hire more masons. Ideally, we can hire 30 masons and finish it in one day. Of course, there are practical limitations to the number of masons we can add, such as the size of the wall, the space in which they are operating together, and the way they access resources, such as clay and bricks. If you put too many cooks in one kitchen, you will end up having the cooks bumping to each other, arguing, trying to keep out of one another's way, without doing much of cooking. A situation like this is called *thrashing*.

Hence the idea is simple: put more CPUs in the machine. *Dual-core* machines have two CPUs (two cores) on the same chip. These CPUs share the same cache (as shown in Figure 1.6) and the rest of the system components.

Laptop and desktop computers with more than two cores are also available nowadays for reasonable prices. Quad-core machines are slowly appearing in the market. Machines with many more cores (8, 16, 32, 64, 128, and more) are expensive and are acquired by large organizations and research institutes.

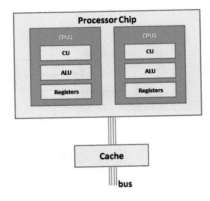

Figure 1.6: Dual-core CPU

Memory hierarchy

A bit represents a **0** or a **1**. A group of 8 bits is called a *byte*. A *Kilobyte* is 1024 bytes. A *Megabyte* is 1024 Kilobytes or 1,048,576 bytes. A *Gigabyte* is 1024 Megabytes or 1,073,741,824 bytes. A *Terabyte* is 1024 Gigabyte or 1,099,511,627,776 bytes.

Memory can be arranged into the hierarchy shown in Figure 1.7. As we go up this hierarchy, the *price per bit* becomes higher. Registers are more expensive than caches, which are more expensive than main memory, which is more expensive than a hard disk, which is more expensive than a DVD. The same applies to *speed*. Things get slower as we move down the hierarchy. For instance, registers are very fast since they are part of the CPU itself. Cache memory is faster than main memory, but slower than registers, and so on. Finally, the *size* shrinks as we go up the hierarchy. Registers are typically several bytes in size; the cache is a few Megabytes in size; main memory is a couple of Gigabytes; a hard disk is a few hundred of Gigabytes; and the pile of CDs and DVDs you have on your desk and inside your drawers is much larger than hundreds of Gigabytes.

Figure 1.7: Memory hierarchy

Magnetic disk operation

A hard disk (Figure 1.8) consists of a collection of double-sided *platters*, typically made from some hard metal (thus the name "hard" disk). These platters are mounted on a *spindle* which spins, rotating with it the platters.

Information is stored on the surfaces of the platters as electro-magnetic signals, which are read and written by *read/write heads*. There is one such head for each surface. A head comes very close to the surface, without touching it, and it can sniff the electro-magnetic signals (reading) or spit them to the surface (writing). The heads are attached to one *arm* that moves inwards and outwards in the direction of the spindle, positioning the heads at a desired radius from the center of the platters. The spindle moves the platters so that the required location on a platter surface falls underneath a read/write head.

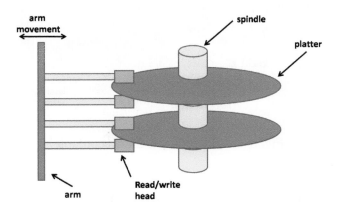

Figure 1.8: Two-platter hard disk

Optical disk operation

Optical disks, such as music CDs and DVDs, do not use electro-magnetic nor electric signals to store information. An optical disk (Figure 1.9) has a thin dye layer of metal protected by a layer of plastic. The bits are literally *burned* into this dye layer. A hot laser beam burns holes into the dye layer, resulting in a spiral structure of *pits* (holes) and *lands* (no holes). Since each can represent a 0 or a 1, a colder laser beam can read this information back, without affecting the dye.

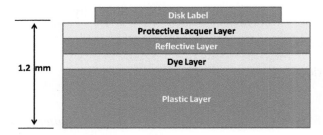

Figure 1.9: Magnified cross-sectional sketch of a CD-Recordable

If the beam escapes the dye layer and is reflected back by the reflective layer, this indicates a 1; if the dye is burnt, resulting in a dark spot, it prevents the beam from reaching the reflective layer and cannot be reflected back. This indicates a 0. This is depicted in Figure 1.10.

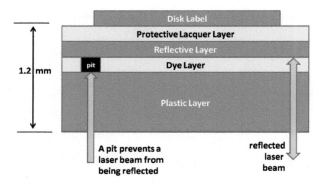

Figure 1.10: Reading a CD-Recordable

How about re-writable disks? A medium hot laser beam can be used to heat the die layer so that all pits disappear. Have you ever heard of dual layer disks? These use two layers of different dyes so that the laser beam, if pointed at the right angle, can get to one of the two layers as if the other layer does not exist.

1.5 Information Coding

Anything can be represented, or *encoded*, as bits, including text and multimedia files. For instance, denoting a wall by 1 and empty space by 0, the robot's world of Figure 1.1 can be represented using bits, as is shown in Figure 1.11.

```
1 1 1 1 1 1 1 1 1 1
1 0 0 0 1 0 1 0 0 1
1 0 0 0 1 0 1 0 0 1
1 0 0 1 1 0 1 0 0 1
1 0 0 0 1 0 1 0 0 1
1 0 0 0 1 0 0 0 0 1
1 0 0 0 0 0 0 0 0 1
1 1 1 1 1 1 1 1 1 1
```

Figure 1.11: The robot's world as a grid of bits

How about the alphabet and other symbols? These are called *characters* and can be encoded with bits using predefined fixed-length codes. One famous way of *encoding* is ASCII (American Standard Code for Information Exchange) codes. ASCII is a convention that assigns to each symbol a fixed code of 0s and 1s. For instance, the ASCII code for character A is 0100 0001, the ASCII code for B is 0100 0010, the ASCII code for C is 0100 0011, the ASCII code for D is 0100 0100, and so on.

An ASCII code is composed of 8 bits; we say the code is of *length* 8. Every character you can type on the keyboard has an ASCII representation, including a space, #, and $.

The word ACE is encoded in ASCII by 010000010100001101000101. To know what a code really represents, read the first 8 digits and find out which character they represent, then read the next 8 and so on. This process is called *decoding*.

ASCII codes can represent 2^8 different characters, which is 256 characters. In general, if you're coding characters with codes each of length n and the coding uses a coding-symbols, you can represent a^n different characters. (In the case of ASCII, $a = 2$ because the codes consist of two coding-symbols 0 and 1, and $n = 8$ because the length of an ASCII code is 8.)

Exercises

1. Sorting a hand of cards in ascending order can be formulated as a problem. Describe this problem by specifying its input and output.

2. Formulate an algorithm for sorting a hand of cards.

3. Finding an exam paper for a particular student in a pile of exam papers can be formulated as a problem. Describe this problem by specifying its input and output.

4. Formulate an algorithm for finding a particular exam paper in a pile of exam papers.

5. Often, you search the Web for some document. In the hit list, you find a brief description of a document that contains a phrase that interests you. You open this document, but you cannot find the phrase that was included in the brief description. Explain why this happens.

6. Physicists know that when they look at stars, they are looking at the history of the universe. Since a star is very far, light takes a long time to reach us. Hence, we do not see a star the way it is right now; we see it the way it was when the light we are seeing now was emitted from the star. Is it true that when we are looking at a search engine database, we are looking at the history of the Web? Justify your answer.

7. Maria is looking into an elective course to take next semester. Her criteria for such a course are: (1) small class size in previous offering and (2) high previous student ratings of the instructor. Both criteria are equally important to Maria. The objective value that Maria is calculating is $50\% \times CLASS\_SIZE + 50\% \times INSTRUCTOR\_RATINGS$. Is this an appropriate way to calculate the objective value? Justify your answer.

8. John would like to buy a new car. His top three criteria are: price, fuel consumption, and durability. He wants low price and fuel consumption but he is interested in a car with high durability. All three criteria are equally important to him. Formulate an appropriate objective value.

9. Awarding Oscars to movies requires taking into consideration different criteria.

    (a) Select three criteria that you think are the most important factors in awarding Oscars.

    (b) Prioritize these three criteria by assigning percentage weights to each of them.

    (c) Create a spreadsheet containing 10 of your favorite movies, assigning to each movie values for the three criteria.

    (d) Devise an objective value formula that is appropriate for selecting Oscar-winning movies.

    (e) Identify the two best movies based on your objective values.

10. The robot that was discussed in this chapter can rotate left or right. Imagine a robot that can only rotate left. Modify the robot's program so that only left rotations are allowed.

11. Is a music CD considered sequential access or random access memory? Justify your answer.

12. What does *volatility* of memory mean? Are flash sticks volatile?

13. Explain the writing and reading operations of double-layer optical disks.

14. Research *solid-state drives* and position them the memory hierarchy.

15. File *f.txt* is stored on a hard disk and contains words only formed of the characters: A, E, B, C, W, and <space>. The file contains 2000 characters.

    (a) Using 8-bit ASCII codes, how many bits are required to encode the file *f.txt*?

    (b) What is the minimum length of codes that can encode all the characters of file *f.txt*?

16. Search the Web for ASCII tables. What are the ASCII codes for <space bar>, #, $, and comma?

17. The representation of the robot's world as a matrix of 0s and 1s gives us an idea how black and white images are represented inside the computer. Search the Web to learn about the representation of colored images. How can these be represented using 0s and 1s?

18. Search the Web to learn about the representation of movies using 0s and 1s. Summarize your findings.

CHAPTER 2

First Things First: Foundations

Logic and sets are central to understanding computer science, and algorithms are the heart of the field. With logic it is possible to formulate unambiguous statements, and the rules of logic facilitate *reasoning*, which is a very important tool. Designing computing devices and constructing computer programs (Chapter 5) require logic and logical reasoning.

Much of computer science is devoted to the study of objects, and set theory provides the foundations for formally representing objects and their relationships. Graphs, trees, finite state machines, (Chapter 3) and databases (Chapter 4) are all founded in set theory. This chapter serves as required background for those later chapters.

2.1 Propositional Logic

A *proposition* is a declarative sentence which must be either *true* or *false*, but not both. True and false are called *truth values*. The area of logic that studies propositions is called *propositional logic* or *propositional calculus*.

Example 2.1

The following statements are propositions:

1. The sun is a star

2. Planet Earth orbits the moon

3. $6 + 5 < 3$

4. $6 + 5 > 3$

Each of these propositions has a truth value. For instance, propositions 1 and 4 are true, but propositions 2 and 3 are false.

The following statements are not propositions:

1. Do you like computers?

2. You should get some sleep.

3. $2x > 12$

The first two sentences are not declarative. The statement $2x > 12$ is worth a little more explanation. It is not possible to determine the truth value of this statement if the value of the variable x is unknown. The statement may be true (for instance when x is 10) and could be false as well (for instance when x is 1). This statement can be converted to a proposition if the value of x is fixed. However, we will see later how to convert it to a proposition without fixing the value of the variable x, using *predicate logic*.

Compound Propositions

Compound propositions can be built by combining one or more propositions, using *logical operators*. There are three major logical operators:

1. Negation, the *not* operator

2. Conjunction, the *and* operator

3. Disjunction, the *or* operator

Example 2.2

The following are compound propositions:

1. Today it is raining, **and** the outside temperature is above 15^oC.

2. At 12:00 today, I will be eating **or** I will be sleeping.

3. Mars is **not** a planet in our solar system.

Negation

If p is a proposition, then $\neg p$ is a proposition that is true when p is false, and it is false when p is true. $\neg p$ is read "not p".

A compound proposition can be defined using a *truth table*, which displays all the combinations of truth values of counterpart propositions. The truth table for negation is given in Table 2.1.

p	$\neg p$
F	T
T	F

Table 2.1: Truth table for negation

Note that $\neg(\neg p)$ is equivalent to p. This is called *double negation*. For instance saying "the earth orbits the sun" is the same as "it is **not** true that the earth does **not** orbit the sun".

Conjunction

If p and q are propositions, then $p \wedge q$ is a proposition that is true when both p and q are true, and it is false when at least one of p or q is false. $p \wedge q$ is read "p and q". The truth table for conjunction is given in Table 2.2.

p	q	$p \wedge q$
F	F	F
F	T	F
T	F	F
T	T	T

Table 2.2: Truth table for conjunction

if one is false, everything's false

Disjunction

If p and q are propositions, then $p \vee q$ is a proposition that is false when both p and q are false, and it is true when at least one of p or q is true. $p \vee q$ is read "p or q". The truth table for disjunction is given in Table 2.3.

p	q	$p \vee q$
F	F	F
F	T	T
T	F	T
T	T	T

Table 2.3: Truth table for disjunction

if one is true, everything's true.

The *or* operator is inclusive. $p \vee q$ simply states that the compound proposition is true if p is true, q is true, or both p and q are true. The statement "to use the elevator, you must be at least 14 years old **or** accompanied by someone who is at least 14 years old" is inclusive. You can be at least 14 and also accompanied by someone who is also at least 14, and both of you can use the elevator.

Often, we use an exclusive version of *or* in our daily logic. The proposition: "I drive **or** walk to school" is exclusive. The counterpart propositions "I drive to school" and "I walk to school" cannot be both true at the same time. If I drive to school, this excludes the possibility that I walk to school, and vice versa. That is, the propositions "I drive to school" and "I walk to school" mutually exclude each other. This gives rise to a fourth logic operator: the *exclusive or* (abbreviated *xor*).

If p and q are propositions, then $p \oplus q$ is a proposition that is true when exactly one of p or q is true, otherwise it is false. $p \oplus q$ is read "p xor q". The truth table for *xor* is given in Table 2.4. Note that the only difference between Table 2.4 and Table 2.3 is in the case when both p and q are true.

p	q	$p \oplus q$
F	F	F
F	T	T
T	F	T
T	T	F

Table 2.4: Truth table for *xor*

Tautologies and contradictions

A *tautology* is a proposition that is always true. A *contradiction* is a proposition that is always false.

The statement "John passed or failed the computer science course" is a tautology. This is the same as saying "John passed the computer science course or John did not passed the computer science course". The simplest tautology is $p \lor \neg p$. This is always true regardless of what the value of p is, as evident in Table 2.5

p	$\neg p$	$p \lor \neg p$
F	T	T
T	F	T

Table 2.5: Truth table for a tautology

The statement "In the 2007-08 season, both the Detroit Red Wings and the Anaheim Ducks won the Stanley Cup" is a contradiction. If the Detroit Red Wings won the cup, then the Anaheim Ducks lost the cup. The statement reduces to saying "in the 2007-08 season, the Anaheim Ducks lost and won the Stanley Cup". The simplest contradiction is $p \land \neg p$. This is always false regardless of the truth value of p is, as evident in Table 2.6

p	$\neg p$	$p \land \neg p$
F	T	F
T	F	F

Table 2.6: Truth table for a contradiction

Logical equivalence

Two compound propositions are said to be *logically equivalent* if they have the same truth values in all possible cases. A truth table can be used to show logical equivalence.

Example 2.3

The $\oplus$ operator can be expressed using the three core operators: $\neg$, $\wedge$, and $\vee$. The proposition $p \oplus q$ is equivalent to $(p \vee q) \wedge \neg(p \wedge q)$ as is shown in Table 2.7. It can be verified from this table that the truth values in columns $[p \oplus q]$ and $[(p \vee q) \wedge \neg(p \wedge q)]$ are the same; hence, the propositions $p \oplus q$ is logically equivalent to $(p \vee q) \wedge \neg(p \wedge q)$.

p	q	$p \oplus q$	$p \vee q$	$p \wedge q$	$\neg(p \wedge q)$	$(p \vee q) \wedge \neg(p \wedge q)$
F	F	F	F	F	T	F
F	T	T	T	F	T	T
T	F	T	T	F	T	T
T	T	F	T	T	F	F

Table 2.7: Truth table showing logical equivalence between $p \oplus q$ and $(p \vee q) \wedge \neg(p \wedge q)$

Table 2.8 shows some famous logical equivalence rules. Their verification using truth tables is left as an exercise.

Law name	Equivalence law
Tautology and Contradiction	$p \vee \neg p = T$
	$p \wedge \neg p = F$
Identity	$p \wedge T = p$
	$p \vee F = p$
Domination	$p \vee T = T$
	$p \wedge F = F$
Idempotent	$p \vee p = p$
	$p \wedge p = p$
Double negation	$\neg(\neg p) = p$
Commutation	$p \vee q = q \vee p$
	$p \wedge q = q \wedge p$
Association	$(p \vee q) \vee r = p \vee (q \vee r)$
	$(p \wedge q) \wedge r = p \wedge (q \wedge r)$
Distribution	$p \wedge (q \vee r) = (p \wedge q) \vee (p \wedge r)$
	$p \vee (q \wedge r) = (p \vee q) \wedge (p \vee r)$
DeMorgan's	$\neg(p \wedge q) = \neg p \vee \neg q$
	$\neg(p \vee q) = \neg p \wedge \neg q$
Implication	$p \rightarrow q = \neg p \vee q$
Contrapositive	$p \rightarrow q = \neg q \rightarrow \neg p$

Table 2.8: Logic equivalence laws

Implication

If p and q are propositions, then $p \to q$ is a proposition that is false when p is true and q is false; otherwise it is true. $p \to q$ is read "p implies q", or "if p then q", or "q only if p". The truth table for implication is given in Table 2.9.

p	q	$p \to q$
F	F	T
F	T	T
T	F	F
T	T	T

FALSE IF,

OTHERWISE,

TRUE

Table 2.9: Truth table for implication

The definition of implication is intriguing. It states that you can start from a false premise and arrive at any conclusion (true or false), but starting from a true premise, you can only arrive at true conclusions.

Example 2.4

Consider the proposition: "If you have a Canadian passport, then you are a Canadian citizen". This proposition is stating that a Canadian passport is proof of Canadian citizenship, and the proposition is true. If we let p = "You have a Canadian passport" and q = "You are a Canadian citizen", then it is clear that this proposition is $p \to q$.

If both p and q are false, then $p \to q$ is true. There is nothing wrong in not having a Canadian passport while you are not a Canadian citizen. In fact, all those who are not Canadian citizens do not have Canadian passports.

When p is false and q is true, then $p \to q$ is also true. If you do not have a Canadian passport, you can still be a Canadian citizen. Not all Canadian citizens have Canadian passports; they only obtain one if they need to travel outside Canada.

When both p and q are true, $p \to q$ is still true. This does not require much explanation. If someone has a Canadian passport and is a Canadian citizen then the statement is true.

The last case is when p is true but q is false. In this case, $p \to q$ is false. It can never be the case that you have a Canadian passport, and at the same time you are not a Canadian citizen. This is impossible and so the proposition $p \to q$ is false in this case.

Just like *xor*, implication is also redundant and can be expressed using the core logical operators: $\neg$, $\wedge$, and $\vee$. The proposition $p \to q$ is logically equivalent to $\neg p \vee q$. Verification of this equivalence using a truth table is left as an exercise.

An implication $p \to q$ is always equivalent to $\neg q \to \neg p$, which is called the *contrapositive* of $p \to q$.

Example 2.5

The proposition: "If you have a Canadian passport, then you are a Canadian citizen" is equivalent to its contrapositive, the proposition "If you are not a Canadian citizen, then you do not have a Canadian passport".

Precedence of logic operators

If a complex proposition does not have brackets such as $\neg p \vee q$, we have to specify precedence rules so that the meaning of the proposition does not result in confusion. For instance, does $\neg p \vee q$ mean $\neg(p \vee q)$ or does it mean $(\neg p) \vee q$? In other words, should we apply negation first and then apply disjunction or vice versa? When there are no brackets, the operators are applied in the following order:

1. $\neg$

2. $\wedge$, $\vee$, and $\oplus$

3. $\rightarrow$

That is, $\neg p \vee q$ means $(\neg p) \vee q$ because $\neg$ has a higher precedence over $\vee$ and is applied first. When operators have equal precedence, they should be applied left to right as they appear in the proposition. For example, $p \vee q \wedge r$ is the same as $(p \vee q) \wedge r$. The $\vee$ is applied first because it is in the same precedence category as $\wedge$ and it occurs first in the proposition. To avoid confusion, it is always a good idea to use brackets as we have been doing in most of our examples.

Truth tables in Microsoft Excel

Microsoft Excel recognizes the truth values, *true* and *false*, as special values. When a truth value is typed into an Excel cell, it is replaced it with an all caps value: TRUE or FALSE. Excel also provides the basic three logic operators: *and*, *or*, and *not*. The format for using these is:
NOT(*a truth value*)
AND(*a list or a range of truth values*)
OR(*a list or a range of truth values*)
The following is an Excel truth table that verifies the DeMorgan's rule $\neg(p \wedge q) = \neg p \vee \neg q$:

	A	B	C	D
1	p	q	not (p and q)	(not p) or (not q)
2	FALSE	FALSE	TRUE	TRUE
3	FALSE	TRUE	TRUE	TRUE
4	TRUE	FALSE	TRUE	TRUE
5	TRUE	TRUE	FALSE	FALSE

The formula in cell $C2$ is =NOT(AND($A2$,$B2$)) and that of cell $D2$ is =OR(NOT($A2$),NOT($B2$)).

2.2   Predicate Logic

We have argued earlier that statements involving variables are not propositions if the value of the variable is unknown. For example, $x > 0$ is not a proposition. A statement of this form is called a *predicate*. A predicate has two parts: the variables involved and the statement about the variables.

Example 2.6

> Let Positive(x) denote the predicate $x > 0$. Positive(1) is true, but Positive(-6) is false.
>
> Let Greater(x, y) denote the predicate $x > y$. Greater$(1, 2)$ is false, but Greater$(2, 1)$ is true.

Predicates can be made propositions by fixing the values of their variables, such as Positive(1). Predicates require a *universe of discourse*, which is the collection of values from which a variable can be fixed. With the predicate Positive(x), the universe of discourse is assumed to be the collection of all numbers. If for instance Fido is a dog, the statement Positive(Fido) does not make any sense. Fido is not in our universe of discourse.

Quantification converts predicates to propositions without fixing the values of the variable. There are two types of quantifiers: *universal* and *existential*.

Universal quantifiers

every or for all

Let $P(x)$ be a predicate, then $\forall x P(x)$ is a proposition that is true when $P(x)$ is true for all the values of x in the universe of discourse; it is false otherwise. $\forall$ is read "every" or "for all".

Example 2.7

> If the universe of discourse is all numbers, then $\forall x$Positive(x) is false because not all numbers are greater than 0.
>
> Let $RW(x) = $ "x can read and write" and $U(x) = $ "x is a university student". If the universe of discourse is all human beings, then the following proposition is true: $\forall x(U(x) \to RW(x))$. In plain English, all humans who are university students can read and write. Note however, that the proposition $\forall x(U(x) \land RW(x))$ is false, since it asserts that all humans are university students and they all can read and write.

Existential quantifiers

*there is
there exists*

Let $P(x)$ be a predicate, then $\exists x P(x)$ is a proposition that is true when $P(x)$ is true for at least one value of x in the universe of discourse; it is false otherwise. $\exists$ is read "there is", "there exists", or "for some".

Example 2.8

If the universe of discourse is all numbers, then $\exists x \text{Positive}(x)$ is true because there exists at least one value in the universe of discourse which is positive.

Let $RW(x) = $ "x can read and write" and $U(x) = $ "x is a university student". If the universe of discourse is all human beings, then the following proposition is false: $\exists x(U(x) \land \neg RW(x))$. The proposition states that there is at least one university student who cannot read or write.

Example 2.9

Let the universe of discourse be all earth creatures. Let $M(x) = $ "x is a monkey" and $F(x) = $ "x lives in a forest". The propositions $\exists x(M(x) \land F(x))$ states that there are some monkeys living in forests, and this proposition is true.

How would we express in logic the statement "all monkeys live in forests"? One common mistake is: $\forall x(M(x) \land F(x))$. This statement says that all earth creatures are monkeys and live in forests! The correct way is: $\forall x(M(x) \rightarrow F(x))$, meaning that from all creatures, if x is a monkey, then x lives in a forest.

Since not all monkeys live in forests, the proposition $\forall x(M(x) \rightarrow F(x))$ is false.

Quantifier equivalence

$\forall x P(x)$ is equivalent to $\neg \exists x \neg P(x)$.
Saying all monkeys are black is the same as saying there is no single monkey which is not black.
$\exists x P(x)$ is equivalent to $\neg \forall x \neg P(x)$.
The statement that "there is at least one person who likes ice cream" is logically the same as the statement "it is not the case that all people do not like ice cream".

2.3 Naive Set Theory

Sets

A _set_ is an unordered collection of unique objects. The objects of a set are called _elements_ or _members_ of the set. The order of objects in a set is irrelevant. Furthermore, the objects in a set must be unique; that is, no element can be repeated in a set.

A small set can be represented by listing its members; for instance, A is the set of all possible choices in the paper-rock-scissors game:

$$A = \{\text{paper}, \text{scissors}, \text{rock}\}$$

B is the set of all chess pieces:

$$B = \{\text{pawn}, \text{knight}, \text{bishop}, \text{rook}, \text{queen}, \text{king}\}$$

C is the set of all positive integers less than or equal to 5 :

$$C = \{1, 2, 3, 4, 5\}$$

It is not always possible to list all members of a set. Some sets are very large, and some are infinite. Large sets can be represented using the set builder notation, such as:

$$A = \{x | x \text{ is a student}\}$$

This set builder notation has two parts, the variable x and the predicate "x is a student". The symbol "$|$" is read "such that". Thus, A is the set of all elements x such that x is a student. Simply, A is the set of all students.

The set of all even numbers is infinite:

$$B = \{x | x \text{ is an even number}\}$$

Sets can be empty. The empty set is represented by $\{\}$ or using the symbol $\emptyset$.

The set $\{\text{paper}, \text{scissors}, \text{rock}\}$ is the same as the set $\{\text{paper}, \text{scissors}, \text{rock}, \text{rock}\}$, since elements of a set should be unique and repetitive elements are counted only once.

The order of members in a set is immaterial: $\{\text{paper}, \text{scissors}, \text{rock}\}$, $\{\text{scissors}, \text{rock}, \text{paper}\}$, and $\{\text{rock}, \text{paper}, \text{scissors}\}$ all represent the same set.

A *multiset* is an unordered collection of objects that are not necessarily unique. That is, a multiset allows the duplication of elements.

Inclusion and membership

Given an element x and a set A, the predicate $x \in A$ states that x is a member of (or belongs to) A. Similarly, $x \notin A$ represents $\neg(x \in A)$. A set A is said to be a subset of set B, written $A \subseteq B$, if all the elements of A are also elements of B. That is, if $\forall x \, (x \in A \rightarrow x in B)$, then $A \subseteq B$.

Example 2.10

$\{1, 2\} \subseteq \{1, 2, 7\}$
$\{1, 2, 5\} \nsubseteq \{1, 2, 7\}$
$\{a\} \subseteq \{\alpha | \alpha \text{ is a letter in the English alphabet}\}$
$a \in \{\alpha | \alpha \text{ is a letter in the English alphabet}\}$
$\{H, I, T\} \subseteq \{H, I, T\}$

$$J \notin \{H, I, T\}$$
$$\emptyset \subseteq \{1, 2, 7\}$$

The empty set, $\emptyset$ is a subset of any set B. Since for any element x, $x \in \emptyset$ is always false, $x \in \emptyset \rightarrow x \in B$ is always true.

Venn diagrams are a pictorial way of representing sets. A set is drawn as an ellipse, inside which the member elements can be indicated. Figures 2.1 and 2.2 depict examples. The universe of values $\mathcal{U}$ from which all the elements of sets are selected is drawn as a surrounding box. That is, every set is a subset of $\mathcal{U}$.

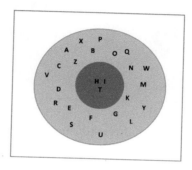

Figure 2.1: Venn diagram showing the $\{H, I, T\}$ as a subset of the capital letters in the English alphabet

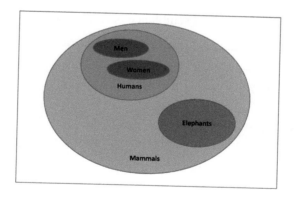

Figure 2.2: Venn diagram showing a partial relationship between mammals, humans, and elephants

Intersection

The set $A \cap B$ is the set of all elements that are common between the sets A and B. More formally, $A \cap B = \{x | x \in A \land x \in B\}$. Note the resemblance between $\cap$ of sets and $\land$ of propositions. If $A \cap B = \emptyset$, then A and B are said to be *disjoint*.

Example 2.11

Let $A = \{1, 6, 8\}$, $B = \{1, 3, 5, 7\}$, and $C = \{3, 5, 7\}$

$A \cap B = \{1\}$

$B \cap C = \{3, 5, 7\} = C$

$A \cap C = \{\}$ or $\emptyset$

Figure 2.3 shows a Venn diagram example with intersection.

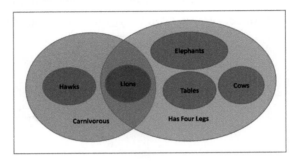

Figure 2.3: Venn diagram showing a partial relationship between carnivorous creatures and four-legged objects

Union

The set $A \cup B$ is the set of all elements that are in the set A plus the elements of B. More formally, $A \cup B = \{x | x \in A \lor x \in B\}$. Note the resemblance between $\cup$ of sets and $\lor$ of propositions.

Example 2.12

Let $A = \{1, 6, 8\}$, $B = \{1, 3, 5, 7\}$, and $C = \{3, 5, 7\}$

$A \cup B = \{1, 3, 5, 6, 7, 8\}$

$B \cup C = \{1, 3, 5, 7\} = B$

$A \cup C = \{1, 3, 5, 6, 7, 8\}$

Difference

The set $A - B$ is the set of all elements that are in the set A but are not elements of B. More formally, $A - B = \{x | x \in A \land x \notin B\}$.

Example 2.13

Let $A = \{1, 6, 8\}$, $B = \{1, 3, 5, 7\}$, and $C = \{3, 5, 7\}$

$A - B = \{6, 8\}$

$B - C = \{1\}$

$C - B = \emptyset$

$C - A = C$

Figure 2.4 shows a Venn diagram example with set difference. The set of "carnivorous animals" minus the set of "four-legged objects" gives us the "carnivorous animals that do not have four legs" such as snakes and hawks.

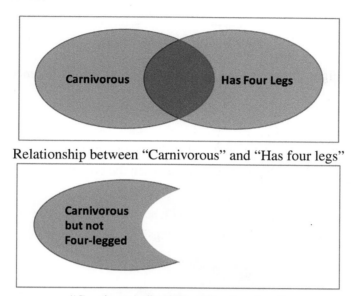

Relationship between "Carnivorous" and "Has four legs"

"Carnivorous" minus "Has four legs"

Figure 2.4: Venn diagram showing carnivorous animals that are not four-legged

Symmetric difference

The symmetric difference of two sets A and B defined as $A \oplus B = (A \cup B) - (A \cap B)$. That is, $A \oplus B$ is the set of elements that are either in A or in B, but not in both. Note the resemblance between $\oplus$ of sets and $\oplus$ of propositions. In fact, the notation $\oplus$ is *overloaded*: when used with sets it means the symmetric difference, but when used with propositions it means *xor*. Hence, the symmetric difference can be defined as: $A \oplus B = \{x | x \in A \oplus x \in B\}$, where the $\oplus$ inside the set definition is the *xor* of the propositions $x \in A$ and $x \in B$.

Example 2.14

Let $A = \{1, 6, 8\}$, $B = \{1, 3, 5, 7\}$, and $C = \{3, 5, 7\}$
$A \cup B = \{1, 3, 5, 6, 7, 8\}$
$A \cap B = \{1\}$
$A \oplus B = \{1, 3, 5, 6, 7, 8\} - \{1\} = \{3, 5, 6, 7, 8\}$
$B \oplus C = \{1\}$

Figure 2.5 shows a Venn diagram example with symmetric difference.

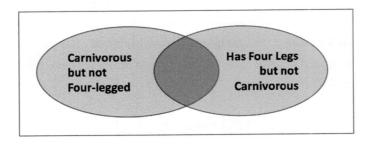

Figure 2.5: Venn diagram showing symmetric difference

Complement

The complement of set A is $\bar{A} = \{x | x \notin A\}$. $\bar{A}$ includes all the elements of $\mathcal{U}$, except those that are in A; that is $\bar{A} = \mathcal{U} - A$. Note the resemblance between the complement of a set and the negation ($\neg$) of a proposition.

Figure 2.6 shows a Venn diagram example with set complement. The complement of the "Has four legs" set is anything that "does not have four legs".

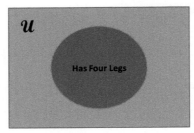

Relationship between the universe and "Has four legs"

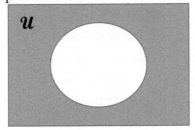

"Does not have four legs"

Figure 2.6: Venn diagram showing the complement of "Has four legs"

Identities

Noting the dualities between logical $\wedge$ and set $\cap$, logical $\vee$ and set $\cup$, and logical $\neg$ and set complement, logical equivalence laws also have duals with sets. For example, DeMorgan's law $\neg(p \wedge q) = \neg p \vee \neg q$ with propositions has its dual $\overline{(A \cap B)} = \bar{A} \cup \bar{B}$ with sets. Set identities can be shown using truth tables, but in the context of sets they are called *membership tables*. In a membership table, complement is interpreted as $\neg$, $\cap$ as $\wedge$, and $\cup$ as $\vee$. The value F means an arbitrary element is not in the set and a T value means otherwise. For instance,

A	B	$A \cap B$
F	F	F

is interpreted as: if an element $x \notin A$ (the proposition $x \in A$ is false) and $x \notin B$, then $x \notin A \cap B$. The identity $\overline{(A \cap B)} = \bar{A} \cup \bar{B}$ is verified in Table 2.10.

A	B	$A \cap B$	$\overline{(A \cap B)}$	$\bar{A}$	$\bar{B}$	$\bar{A} \cup \bar{B}$
F	F	F	T	T	T	T
F	T	F	T	T	F	T
T	F	F	T	F	T	T
T	T	T	F	F	F	F

Table 2.10: Membership table showing DeMorgan's $\overline{(A \cap B)} = \bar{A} \cup \bar{B}$

The identity rules for sets are summarized in Table 2.11. The table also lists the dual logical identities. Note the duality between F and $\emptyset$ and between T and $\mathcal{U}$.

Ordered tuples

We use curly brackets (braces) to represent sets in which the order of elements is immaterial; for instance, {rock, paper} is the same set as {paper, rock}. If the order of members is important, we use *ordered tuples*. Ordered tuples are listed between parentheses, such as (rock, paper). Note that (rock, paper) $\neq$ (paper, rock). Here the order of elements is important. For example, these pairs could be representing the move choices in the paper-scissors-rock game of two players. (rock, paper) would mean that player 1's choice is rock, and player 2's choice is paper, while (paper, rock) would mean the opposite.

A tuple of size n has the general form: $(v_1, v_2, v_3, \ldots, v_n)$. We only consider tuples that have a finite size (n is finite). In tuples, repetition of elements is allowed. For instance, the tuple $(90, 85, 90, 80, 95)$ could be the project grades corresponding to the members of a team of five students. Students 1 and 3 have the same grade.

Name	Set Identity Law	Dual Logical Equivalence Law
Complementation	$A \cup \bar{A} = \mathcal{U}$ $A \cap \bar{A} = \emptyset$	$p \vee \neg p = \text{T}$ $p \wedge \neg p = \text{F}$
Identity	$A \cup \emptyset = A$ $A \cap \mathcal{U} = A$	$p \vee \text{F} = p$ $p \wedge \text{T} = p$
Domination	$A \cup \mathcal{U} = \mathcal{U}$ $A \cap \emptyset = \emptyset$	$p \vee \text{T} = \text{T}$ $p \wedge \text{F} = \text{F}$
Idempotent	$A \cup A = A$ $A \cap A = A$	$p \vee p = p$ $p \wedge p = p$
Double Complementation	$\bar{\bar{A}} = A$	$\neg(\neg p)) = p$
Commutation	$A \cup B = B \cup A$ $A \cap B = B \cap A$	$p \vee q = q \vee p$ $p \wedge q = q \wedge p$
Association	$(A \cup B) \cup C = A \cup (B \cup C)$ $(A \cap B) \cap C = A \cap (B \cap C)$	$(p \vee q) \vee r = p \vee (q \vee r)$ $(p \wedge q) \wedge r = p \wedge (q \wedge r)$
Distribution	$A \cap (B \cup C) = (A \cap B) \cup (A \cap C)$ $A \cup (B \cap C) = (A \cup B) \cap (A \cup C)$	$p \wedge (q \vee r) = (p \wedge q) \vee (p \wedge r)$ $p \vee (q \wedge r) = (p \vee q) \wedge (p \vee r)$
DeMorgan's	$\overline{(A \cap B)} = \bar{A} \cup \bar{B}$ $\overline{(A \cup B)} = \bar{A} \cap \bar{B}$	$\neg(p \wedge q) = \neg p \wedge \neg q$ $\neg(p \wedge q) = \neg p \vee \neg q$

Table 2.11: Set identities and their dual logical equivalences

Cartesian product

The set $A \times B = \{(a,b) | a \in A \wedge b \in B\}$ is called the *Cartesian product* of the sets A and B. In general $A_1 \times A_2 \times \ldots \times A_n = \{(a_1, a_2, \cdots, a_n) | a_1 \in A_1, a_2 \in A_2, \cdots, \wedge a_n \in A_n\}$.

Example 2.15

Let $A = \{a\}$ and $B = \{1, 2\}$
$A \times B = (a, 1), (a, 2)$

Let $A = \{\text{player1}, \text{player2}\}$ and $B = \{\text{paper}, \text{scissors}, \text{rock}\}$
$A \times B = \{(\text{player1}, \text{paper}), (\text{player1}, \text{scissors}), (\text{player1}, \text{rock}), (\text{player2}, \text{paper}),$
$\qquad (\text{player2}, \text{scissors}), (\text{player2}, \text{rock})\}$

Example 2.16

Let $A = \{s, 3, F, 4\}$ and $B = \{s, F, h, 8\}$
$A \cap B = B \cap A = \{s, F\}$
$A \cup B = B \cup A = \{s, 3, F, 4, h, 8\}$

$$A - B = \{3, 4\}; B - A = \{h, 8\}$$
$$A \times B = \{(s, s), (s, F), (s, h), (s, 8), (3, s), (3, F), (3, h), (3, 8), (F, s), (F, F), (F, h),$$
$$(F, 8), (4, s), (4, F), (4, h), (4, 8)\}$$
$$B \times A = \{(s, s), (s, 3), (s, F), (s, 4), (F, s), (F, 3), (F, F), (F, 4), (h, s), (h, 3), (h, F),$$
$$(h, 4), (8, s), (8, 3), (8, F), (8, 4)\}$$
$$(A \cup B) - (A \cap B) = \{s, 3, F, 4, h, 8\} - \{s, F\} = \{3, 4, h, 8\}$$
$$(A \cap B) - (A \cup B) = \{s, F\} - \{s, 3, F, 4, h, 8\} = \emptyset$$
$$(A - B) \cap (B - A) = \{3, 4\} \cap \{h, 8\} = \emptyset$$
$$(A - B) \cup (B - A) = \{3, 4, h, 8\}$$

Relations

A *relation* from set A to set B is a subset of $A \times B$. In general, A relation on the sets $A_1, A_2, \ldots, A_n$ is a subset of $A_1 \times A_2 \times \ldots \times A_n$. A relation could be defined on a single set: A relation on set A is a subset of $A \times A$.

Example 2.17

Let O be a set of objects and P be a set of properties as follows:

$O = \{$book, lion, plate$\}$ and $P = \{$colored, made-from-paper, has-bones, contains-glass$\}$.
Then, an association of the objects in O with the properties of P is a relation R from O to P:

$R = \{($book, colored$)$, (book, made-from-paper$)$, (lion, has-bones$)$, (plate, colored$)$,
(plate, made-from-paper$)$, (plate, contains-glass$)\}$.

Example 2.18

Let $P = \{$Debra, Ali, John, Mike, Sarah, Alicia$\}$
The set Likes $= \{($Debra, Ali$)$, (Debra, Sarah$)$, (Sarah, John$)$, (John, Alicia$)$, (John, Mike$)$,
(Ali, Sarah$)\}$ is a relation on P. That is, Likes $\subseteq P \times P$.

Let A be a set and R be a relation on A. R can be visually represented as a graph. The Likes relation is represented by the graph of Figure 2.7.

Let A be a set and R a relation on A ($R \subseteq A \times A$). R is *symmetric* when $\forall a, b \in A[(a, b) \in R \rightarrow (b, a) \in R]$. In other words, a symmetric relation is reciprocal.

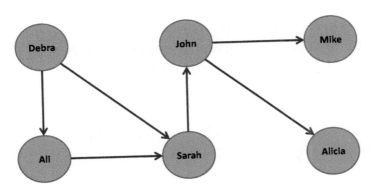

Figure 2.7: Graph representation of the Likes relation

Example 2.19

Let $P = \{1, 4, 67, 90\}$

Let R be the relation "less than" on P.

That is, $R = \{(1, 4), (1, 67), (1, 90), (4, 67), (4, 90), (67, 90)\}$

R is not symmetric, since $1 < 4$ (i.e., $(1, 4) \in R$) does not imply that $4 < 1$. On the contrary, $(1, 4) \in R$ implies that $(4, 1) \notin R$.

Example 2.20

Let $P = \{$Debra, Ali, Sam, Doug, Sarah, Alicia, Samia$\}$, the relation "starts with the same letter" is defined as: $R = \{$(Debra, Doug), (Doug, Debra), (Ali, Alicia), (Alicia, Ali), (Sam, Sarah), (Sarah, Sam), (Sarah, Samia), (Samia, Sarah), (Samia, Sam), (Sam, Samia)$\}$.

R is symmetric: if a and b are two names in P, then "a starts with the same letter as b" $\rightarrow$ "b starts with the same letter as a" for any two names a and b.

For brevity, we replace the ordered pairs (a, b) and (b, a) in a symmetric relation by one pair $\{a, b\}$ and we use braces to indicate that the order $\{a, b\}$ or $\{b, a\}$ is not important. For instance, $R = \{\{$Debra, Doug$\}, \{$Ali, Alicia$\}, \{$Sam, Sarah$\}, \{$Sarah, Samia$\}, \{$Sam, Samia$\}\}$.

In the graph of a symmetric relation, we drop the arrows from the edges (Figure 2.8). Graphs will be studied in more detail in Chapter 3.

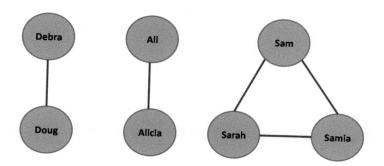

Figure 2.8: Graph representation of a symmetric relation

Spreadsheets & relations

Spreadsheets are relations. Consider the spreadsheet that was developed in Chapter 1:

	A	B	C	D	E
1	State	Avg high temperature	HomicideRate	Time to Ottawa	Objective Value
2	Alabama	33	12	20.37	49.826
3	California	33.44	8.8	41	47.432
4	Connecticut	29.33	3.9	7.12	55.425
5	Georgia	33.44	8.7	18.26	52.03
6	Ilinois	30.6	9.8	15.19	51.242
7	Kansas	33.8	6.1	21.7	52.75
8	Louisiana	34	16.1	25	47.15
9	Maine	26	1.8	17.13	53.474
10	Maryland	30.6	10.9	9.13	51.904
11	Minnesota	28.55	2.8	19.7	53.225
12	Mississippi	33.6	14.2	22.27	48.526
13	Nebraska	31.94	3.9	20.11	53.61
14	New Hampshire	28.11	2.2	6.13	56.107
15	New York	29.61	6.3	5.25	54.683
16	South Dakota	30.27	3	25	52.581

Each row in this spreadsheet is a tuple. For instance, row number 2 is the tuple (Alabama, 33, 12, 20.37, 49.826). The whole table in this sheet is the relation containing all these tuples.

Functions

A *function* f from set A to set B, denoted $f : A \longrightarrow B$, is a relation from A to B with the property: there is exactly one pair $(a, b) \in f$ for each $a \in A$. We write $f(a) = b$ when $(a, b) \in f$. a is the *argument* of f, and b is the *return value*.

Example 2.21

Let $A = \{1, 2, 3\}$ and $B = \{\text{yes}, \text{no}\}$.

The relation $\{(1, \text{yes}), (2, \text{yes}), (3, \text{no})\}$ is a function.

The relation $\{(1, \text{yes}), (2, \text{yes}), (2, \text{no}), (3, \text{no})\}$ is not a function, since there is more than one pair whose first element is 2.

The relation $\{(1, \text{yes}), (2, \text{yes})\}$ is not a function, since there is no pair that starts with 3.

Example 2.22

If A is the set of students in the computer science class and B is the set of grades, the assignment of the course final grades to students is a function from A to B. Notice that every student must have a final grade and a student cannot have more than one final grade (in the same course).

Functions in Microsoft Excel

Microsoft Excel provides a large number of functions that are ready to use in a spreadsheet. For instance, the *and*, *or*, and *not* logic operates in Excel are implemented as functions. An Excel function requires a list of *parameters* or *arguments*. The NOT function requires a single parameter, such as NOT($B12$). Below are some examples of Excel functions:

Function name	Parameters	Description	Examples
SUM	a range of values	the sum of the values in the range	SUM($B2 : B15$) SUM($C2, B2, B3$)
AVERAGE	a range of values	the average the values in the range	AVERAGE($B2 : B15$) AVERAGE($C2, B2, B3$)
COUNT	a range of values	the number of number-values in the range	COUNT($B2 : B15$) COUNT($C2, B2, B3$)
MAX	a range of values	the maximum in the range	MAX($B2 : B15$) MAX($C2, B2, B3$)
MIN	a range of values	the minimum in the range	MIN($B2 : B15$) MIN($C2, B2, B3$)
IF	logical-test, v_1, v_2	returns v_1 if logical-test is true; otherwise, it returns v_2	IF($B2 < C2, C2, 0$) IF($C2 < 0$, "negative", "positive")

2.4 Algorithms

A *problem* is a specification of the relationship between *input* and *output*. If we look at cooking as a problem, the input is some ingredients and the output is edible food. Doing laundry has the input of dirty clothes and the output of clean clothes.

Computational problems are those that are supposed to be carried out or solved by computers. Cooking and doing laundry are not computational, at least not yet, but it will not be too long before computers take part in such problems.

The problem does not specify how the input is converted to output, it simply specifies *what* needs to be done. An *algorithm*, on the other hand, specifies *how* the problem is solved. That is, it specifies how the input is converted to output. An algorithm is a sequence of instructions that transform a given input to a required output.

Algorithms are specific to computational problems. Strictly speaking, a cooking recipe is not an algorithm, simply because it cannot be carried out by a typical computer. However, this distinction between computational and non-computational problems is not important for our purpose. So feel free to consider a cooking recipe or the steps you follow to brush your teeth as algorithms.

Example 2.23

Making Hummus is a problem that converts the input: chickpeas (one cup), smashed garlic (two gloves), lemon juice (1/3 of a cup), salt (1/2 teaspoon), and Tahina sauce (1/3 of a cup) to the output: a delicious Hummus dip.

An algorithm to make Hummus is:

1. Marinate the chickpeas overnight with water

2. Boil the chickpeas until they are very soft

3. Drain the water

4. Add the rest of the ingredients and mix

5. Use a food processor to turn into a paste

Finding the minimum value in a set is a problem whose input is a finite set and the output is the smallest value in a set (assuming we can compare the elements in the set).

For instance if the input is $\{21, 3, 56, 778, 2\}$, the output is 2; or if the input is $\{$James, Alice, Wong, Bob, Samia$\}$ the output is Alice, since Alice is lexicographically (dictionary order) the smallest.

An attempt for an algorithm to find the minimum value in a finite set S is given next.

Set minimum algorithm attempt

Given a finite set S:

1. Let the first element in S be the min-so-far

2. *Check if the next element is less than min-so-far*

   - *If so, make it the min-so-far*

   - *If not, ignore it*

3. *Repeat step 2 until all elements in S are examined*

4. *The minimum is in min-so-far, stop*

We must however, reject this attempt as a solution to the problem at hand as will be explained shortly.

Correctness of algorithms

Algorithms are eventually converted to programs that are executed by computers. So, they have to be explicit, spelling out every relevant detail. An algorithm must always generate the correct output for any legitimate input. The previous algorithm attempt for finding the minimum value in a set does not work if the input set is empty, since there is no first element in an empty set. So, step 1 that considers the first element in an empty set becomes cumbersome. The algorithm also fails if the input is a singleton set, a set containing one element only. In this case, min-so-far will be assigned the only element in the set, but step 2 becomes problematic since the set has no next element.

Though these are the only cases when the algorithm attempt fails, we cannot accept it as a solution. Thus, we have been refraining from calling it an algorithm (we called it an algorithm *attempt*, instead). A correct algorithm must always *terminate*, producing the correct output for any legitimate input.

An algorithm to find the minimum value in a finite set S is: 2.1

Algorithm 2.1. — $Min(S)$ ————————————————————————
Input: *set S*
Output: *minimum element in S*

1. *If $S = \emptyset$, then stop, there is no minimum*

2. *Otherwise (S is non-empty), let the first element in S be the min-so-far*

3. *Repeat the following until all elements in S are examined:*
   Check if the next element is less than min-so-far:

   - *If so, make it the min-so-far*

   - *If not, ignore it*

4. *The minimum is in min-so-far, stop*

Min(S) always terminates (stops looking for the minimum) since the argument S is finite. When it terminates, min-so-far contains the value of the minimum value of S as long as $S \neq \emptyset$. Note how we used function notation to specify Min(S). Indeed, Min(S) is a function from the set of all finite sets with comparable members to the set of all values. If FS is the set of finite sets, then

$$\text{Min} : FS \longrightarrow (\{fs_1\} \cup \{fs_2\} \cup \cdots \cup \{fs_n\}),$$

where $fs_i \subseteq FS$ and $1 \leq i \leq n$. Min(S) is correct: it always finds the minimum element in any legitimate input set S. In the case when $S = \emptyset$, the algorithm terminates, and the minimum does not exist.

Example 2.24

Here we illustrate the operation of Min($\{5, 4, 2, 8, 3\}$), that is $S = \{5, 4, 2, 8, 3\}$.

1. If $S = \emptyset$, then stop, there is no minimum

   S is not empty, so step 1 does not apply and we move to step 2

2. Otherwise (S is non-empty), let the first element in S be the min-so-far

   min-so-far is 5, the first element in the set

3. Repeat the following until all elements in S are examined:

   Only 5 has been examined; the set still has $\{4, 2, 8, 3\}$ unexamined

   Check if the next element is less than min-so-far. If so, make it the min-so-far. If not, ignore it

   The next element is 4; it is less than 5

   The min-so-far becomes 4

3. Repeat the following until all elements in S are examined:

   The set still has $\{2, 8, 3\}$ unexamined

   Check if the next element is less than min-so-far. If so, make it the min-so-far. If not, ignore it

   The next element is 2; it is less than 4

   The min-so-far becomes 2

3. Repeat the following until all elements in S are examined:

   The set still has $\{8, 3\}$ unexamined

   Check if the next element is less than min-so-far. If so, make it the min-so-far. If not, ignore it

The next element is 8; it is not less than 2

8 is ignored; the min-so-far stays 2

3. Repeat the following until all elements in S are examined:

The set still has $\{3\}$ unexamined

Check if the next element is less than min-so-far. If so, make it the min-so-far. If not, ignore it

The next element is 3; it is not less than 2

The min-so-far stays 2

3. Repeat the following until all elements in S are examined:

All elements in the set have been examined; stop

Specifying algorithms

An algorithm can be specified in different ways. One way is to write the algorithm as a program using a language that the computer understands, called *programming language*. Keep in mind that before algorithms are executed by a computer, they must be written in code (as programs). However, one popular way to write algorithms is using *pseudo-code*, which can be as detailed as code, but also includes English sentences. The algorithms that we have considered so far are all in pseudo-code. Before we implement the algorithm on a computer, we write it using pseudo-code so that we can prove or verify certain properties about it. For instance, we need to know if the algorithm is correct before we decide on a programming language. Algorithms can also be specified visually, using *flow-charts*. This will be studied later in the book.

Algorithms can be made more concrete by introducing helpful notation. Algorithm Min() is quite narrative, and it is sometimes desirable to specify it in a better way. This is more desirable for complex algorithms. In the next example algorithm, we will show how to make use of clearer, less narrative pseudo-code.

We would like to specify an algorithm to find whether a particular element x is in a (finite) tuple T. The algorithm "returns" true if $x \in T$ (note that we have overloaded the $\in$ notation to also apply it to tuples); otherwise, it "returns" false. We introduce some notation to refer to elements in the tuple T by specifying their positions. $T[i]$ indicates the element that is at position or *index i* in the tuple. In computer science, numbering starts at 0. For instance, if $T = (a, b, c)$, then $T[0] = a$, $T[1] = b$, and $T[2] = c$. $T[3]$ is undefined since there is no element at index 3 in T. For the empty tuple λ, $\lambda[i]$ is always undefined for any i.

Let T be a set and x be an element, the algorithm Find(x, T) is specified next.

Algorithm 2.2. — *Find*(x, T) ─────────────────────────────

Input: *value x and tuple T*

Output: *true if $x \in T$; false otherwise*

1. *Let i be 0*

2. *If $T[i]$ is undefined,* **return** false

3. *Otherwise if $T[i] = x$, then* **return** true

4. *Otherwise increment i by 1 and repeat steps 2- 4.*
───

The **return** causes the algorithm to behave like a mathematical function. Recall that functions return values. For instance, the function call Power$(2, 2)$ returns the value $2^2 = 4$. The function call 4! returns 24. The call Find$(2, (1, 2, 3))$ returns *true*, but the call Find$(c, (b, a, d))$ returns *false*. The **return** causes the execution of the algorithm to stop. The steps of Find$(2, (1, 2, 3))$ are illustrated in Example 2.25, and the steps of Find$(c, (b, a, d))$ are illustrated in Example 2.26.

Example 2.25 ───────────────────────────────────────

The steps followed when Find$(2, (1, 2, 3))$ is called are as follows:

1. Let i be 0

   i is initialized to 0

2. If $T[i]$ is undefined, **return** *false*

   $T[0]$ is defined and it is equal to 1; the algorithm does not return *false*;

   The algorithm continues with the following step

3. Otherwise if $T[i] = x$, then **return** *true*

   $T[0]$ is not equal to 2; the algorithm does not return *true*;

   The algorithm continues with the following step

4. Otherwise increment i by 1 and repeat steps 2- 4.

   i is incremented to 1; the algorithm continues from step 2

2. If $T[i]$ is undefined, **return** *false*

   $T[1]$ is defined and it is equal to 2; the algorithm does not return *false*;

> The algorithm continues with the following step

3. Otherwise if $T[i] = x$, then **return** *true*

> $T[1]$ is equal to 2; the algorithm returns *true* and terminates

---

Example 2.26

The steps followed when Find$(c, (b, a, d))$ is called are as follows:

1. Let i be 0

> i is initialized to 0

2. If $T[i]$ is undefined, **return** *false*

> $T[0]$ is defined and it is equal to b; the algorithm does not return *false*;

> The algorithm continues with the following step

3. Otherwise if $T[i] = x$, then **return** *true*

> $T[0]$ is not equal to c; the algorithm does not return *true*;

> The algorithm continues with the following step

4. Otherwise increment i by 1 and repeat steps 2- 4.

> i is incremented to 1; the algorithm continues from step 2

2. If $T[i]$ is undefined, **return** *false*

> $T[1]$ is defined and it is equal to a; the algorithm does not return *false*;

> The algorithm continues with the following step

3. Otherwise if $T[i] = x$, then **return** *true*

> $T[1]$ is not equal to c; the algorithm does not return *true*;

> The algorithm continues with the following step

4. Otherwise increment i by 1 and repeat steps 2- 4.

   i is incremented to 2; the algorithm continues from step 2

2. If $T[i]$ is undefined, **return** *false*

   $T[2]$ is defined and it is equal to d; the algorithm does not return *false*;

   The algorithm continues with the following step

3. Otherwise if $T[i] = x$, then **return** *true*

   $T[2]$ is not equal to c; the algorithm does not return *true*;

   The algorithm continues with the following step

4. Otherwise increment i by 1 and repeat steps 2- 4.

   i is incremented to 3; the algorithm continues from step 2

2. If $T[i]$ is undefined, **return** *false*

   $T[3]$ is undefined; the algorithm returns *false* and terminates

---

Efficiency of algorithms

The correctness of an algorithm is a must, but it is also desirable to have efficient algorithms. Efficiency has many dimensions: Is the algorithm fast? Does it require a lot of memory? Does it produce too many messages? etc. Here, we limit our discussion to *time-efficiency*. That is, we desire (but do not necessarily require) algorithms to be as fast as possible. The amount of work an algorithm does determines how long it takes it to solve a given problem. The more work it does, the slower we expect it to be. A good approximation of the time-efficiency of an algorithm would be the number of steps carried out.

For instance, Min($\{5, 4, 2, 8, 3\}$) required 12 steps to find the minimum (see Example 2.24). For larger input, more steps are required to find the minimum. Consequently, the larger the input, the slower the algorithm. Searching through a set of 100 elements will require 3 (steps 1-3) $+100 \times 2$ (steps 4 and 5 repeated for 100 elements) $+1$ (step 6) = 204 steps. To search a set of size n, the algorithm requires $2n + 4$ steps. That is, the time-efficiency of Min(S) is *linearly* proportional to the number of elements in S, the size of the input. Similarly, we can argue that the steps of Find() or Rec_Find() are linear functions of n, where n is the number of elements in the set.

The efficiency of algorithms is used in comparative terms, so that if you're choosing between two algorithms that solve the same problem, you may want to give preference to the faster one. The remaining part of this section demonstrates how one algorithm can be favorable over another.

A medieval merchant learns that one of his 4096 gold coins is fake. The fake coin is visually indistinguishable from the real coins, but since it is made of painted tin, it is lighter than gold. Using a two-pan balance, the merchant needs an efficient algorithm to find the fake coin. Let S be the set of all 4096 coins.

Algorithm 2.3. — *Fake_Coin1(S)* ⎯⎯⎯⎯⎯⎯⎯⎯⎯⎯⎯⎯⎯⎯⎯⎯

Input: *set of coins S, containing one fake coin*

Output: *the fake coin in S*

1. *Choose a pair of coins and scale them on the two-pan balance*
   If one is lighter than the other, stop; the fake coin is found (it is the lighter one)
   If they are of equal weights, put them in the treasure box (they are real gold coins)

2. *Repeat step 1 until there are no more coins*

One way to assess the efficiency of this algorithm is to count the number of balance operations, since the total number of steps carried out is directly proportional to the number of balance operations made. We may be lucky and find the fake coin from the first few trials. However, with algorithm efficiency we prefer to determine the worst-case scenario. This way we can be sure that the algorithm cannot perform any worse than the worst-case. The worst-case scenario is when the fake coin is weighed last.

Since the algorithm weighs the coins in pairs, it needs in the worst-case scenario $4096/2 = 2048$ scaling (or balance) operations. Even if each balance operation takes only 10 seconds, that is $2048 \times 10 = 20480$ seconds, which is close to 6 hours of continuous scaling.

If we have an easy and quick way to divide the coins into equal piles, we can formulate an algorithm that determines the fake coin in 12 balance operations only, even in the worst case.

Algorithm 2.4. — *Fake_Coin2(S)* ⎯⎯⎯⎯⎯⎯⎯⎯⎯⎯⎯⎯⎯⎯⎯⎯

Input: *set of coins S, containing one fake coin*

Output: *the fake coin in S*

1. *Divide the coins into two equal piles*

2. *Balance the two piles on the two-pan balance; one of the piles must be lighter than the other*
   Put the heavier pile in the treasury box; this is a safe pile
   Divide the lighter pile into two equal piles

3. *Repeat step 2 with the new smaller piles, until no more piles can be formed*

The balance steps of Fake_Coin2(S) are as follows:

1. Weigh 2048 coins against 2048 coins, pick the lighter pile and divide it into two equal piles

2. Weigh 1024 coins against 1024 coins, pick the lighter pile and divide it into two equal piles

3. Weigh 512 coins against 512 coins , pick the lighter pile and divide it into two equal piles

4. Weigh 256 coins against 256 coins, pick the lighter pile and divide it into two equal piles

5. Weigh 128 coins against 128 coins, pick the lighter pile and divide it into two equal piles

6. Weigh 64 coins against 64 coins, pick the lighter pile and divide it into two equal piles

7. Weigh 32 coins against 32 coins, pick the lighter pile and divide it into two equal piles

8. Weigh 16 coins against 16 coins, pick the lighter pile and divide it into two equal piles

9. Weigh 8 coins against 8 coins, pick the lighter pile and divide it into two equal piles

10. Weigh 4 coins against 4 coins, pick the lighter pile and divide it into two equal piles

11. Weigh 2 coins against 2 coins, pick the lighter pile and divide it into two equal piles

12. Weigh 1 coin against 1 coin, pick the lighter coin

A few things are worth highlighting with Fake_Coin2(). First, what if the coins cannot be divided into two equal piles? A small modification of the algorithm makes it work regardless of the number of coins. Second, the larger the number of coins, the more beneficial Fake_Coin2() is over Fake_Coin1(). For instance, doubling 4096 coins to 8184 adds one balance operation to Fake_Coin2(), but adds 2048 balance operations to Fake_Coin1(). That is, doubling the coins to 8184 adds 10 seconds to Fake_Coin2(), but it adds 6 more hours to Fake_Coin1()! Finally, the conclusion that Fake_Coin2() is faster than Fake_Coin1() is conditional on having a way to do the division into piles that is faster than 2048 balance operations.

Exercises

1. Use truth tables to show the correctness of the equivalence laws of Table 2.8.

2. What are the truth values of the following propositions?

    (a) If you get an A, then you pass the course.

    (b) If you pass the course, then you get an A.

    (c) If you're a citizen, then you vote in elections.

    (d) If you do not pass the course, then you do not get an A.

3. Write logical expressions for the following propositions. The universe of discourse is all human beings.

    (a) All men are mortal.
       Use the dictionary $M(x) : x$ is a man, $O(x) :$ is mortal

    (b) Some women are immortal.
       Use the dictionary $W(x) : x$ is a woman, $O(x) :$ is mortal

    (c) All monkeys live in forests or zoos.
       Use the dictionary $M(x) : x$ is a monkey, $F(x) : x$ lives in a forest, $Z(x) : x$ lives in a zoo

4. Under which conditions are the propositions $\forall x(P(x) \land Q(x))$ and $\exists x(P(x) \land Q(x))$ equivalent?

5. Under which conditions are the propositions $\forall x(P(x) \rightarrow Q(x))$ and $\forall x(P(x) \land Q(x))$ equivalent?

6. Using a membership table, prove the *absorption laws*:

    (a) $A \cup (A \cap B) = A$
    (b) $A \cap (A \cup B) = A$

7. Which of the following relations on the set of people are symmetric?

    (a) "is taller than"
    (b) "has the same birthday as"
    (c) "is married to"
    (d) "is younger than"

8. Which of the following relations from the set of people to the set of countries are functions?

    (a) "has visited"

(b) "is a citizen of"

(c) "was born in"

9. Write an algorithm that determines if two input tuples are equal or not.

10. Write an algorithm that determines if one input set is a subset of another input set.

11. Write an algorithm that determines if two sets are equal.

12. Write an algorithm that finds the union of two sets.

13. Write an algorithm that finds the intersection of two sets.

14. Write an algorithm that finds the difference of two sets.

15. Write an algorithm that finds the symmetric difference of two sets.

16. Assume that the medieval merchant knows that the fake coin is of a different weight than a real gold coin; however, he does not know if it is lighter or heavier than a real coin. Modify the Fake_Coin2() algorithm so that the merchant can find the fake coin under this assumption.

17. Modify the Fake_Coin2() algorithm so that it works even if the number of coins is not a power of 2.

CHAPTER 3

Abstract Thinking: Graphs & Trees

When designing an algorithm to solve a given computational problem, the representation of the problem can make a big difference. When a problem is formulated using an appropriate model, it makes the formulation of the solution much easier. In Chapter 1, a computational problem was defined as a specification of the relationship of input and output. How input or output is represented and modeled is at the heart of modeling the problem itself.

This chapter introduces *graphs*, basic graph terminology, and few graph algorithms. Graphs can be utilized to represent a large class of computational problems. *Trees* are a special case of graphs that are also extremely popular in computer science. The chapter also introduces trees in addition to information coding as an application of trees. *Finite State Machines* (abbreviated FSM) are introduced in this chapter as graphs with a special meaning. FSMs are very useful when designing hardware tasks, which is sometimes called hardware algorithms.

3.1   Graphs

A *graph* is simply a graphical representation of a relation defined on a set. It has a set of elements, called vertices and a set of edges that connect these vertices. Formally, a graph is a pair of sets, $G = (V_G, E_G)$, where V_G is a set of vertices and the edges $E_G \subseteq V_G \times V_G$ (that is, E_G is a relation on V_G).

If the relation E_G is not symmetric, the edges are one-way and the graph is called a *directed graph*. If the relation E_G is symmetric, the edges are two-way and the graph is *undirected*. It is sometimes also possible to label the edges, and the resulting graph is called a *labeled* graph.

Example 3.1

The graph G_1 in Figure 3.1 has $V_{G_1} = \{A, B, C, D\}$ and $E_{G_1} = \{\{A, B\}, \{A, C\}, \{A, D\}, \{B, C\}\}$. The vertices are drawn as circles and the edges are two-way (there is no indication on the edge that forces it to flow in one direction rather than the other). Note that we have used set notation to indicate undirected edges. So, $\{A, B\}$ is the same edge as $\{B, A\}$. E is a symmetric relation.

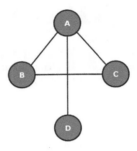

Figure 3.1: Undirected graph G_1

Example 3.2

The graph G_2 in Figure 3.2 has $V_{G_2} = \{A, B, C, D, E, F\}$ and the set of edges $E_{G_2} = \{(A, B), (A, D), (B, A), (B, C), (C, A), (C, F), (D, E), (E, A), (E, E), (F, E)\}$. The edges are one-way, indicated by arrows. Note that in the set E_{G_2}, we used ordered pairs to indicate one-way edges. (A, B) indicates that there is an edge from A to B, but there is also the pair (B, A) indicating another one-way edge from B to A. E is not a symmetric relation. Note also the edge (E, E) from E to itself.

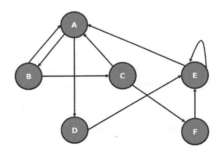

Figure 3.2: Directed graph G_2

Example 3.3

Figure 3.3 shows an example of a labeled graph.

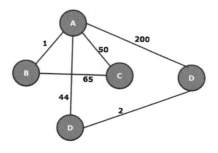

Figure 3.3: A labeled graph

Undirected graph terminology

Two vertices in an undirected graph are called *adjacent* if they are connected by an edge. In graph G_1 (Figure 3.1), A is adjacent to B, C, and D; however, C and D are not adjacent. A (undirected) path is a tuple of vertices $(v_1, v_2, \cdots, v_n)$, such that v_1 is adjacent to v_2, and v_2 is adjacent to v_3, and so on. In G_1, there is a path from D to C, which is (D, A, B, C). Notice that this is not the only path from D to C. A path is called a *cycle* or a *circuit* if $v_1 = v_n$, or, in other words, if it starts and ends at the same vertex. In G_1, the path (A, B, C, A) is a circuit. The *degree* of a vertex is the number of adjacent vertices it has. Hence, the degree of A in G_1 is 3 since it has three adjacent vertices. The degree of B is 2 and that of D is 1. A *connected* graph is a graph that has a path between every pair of its vertices. In this book, we are concerned most of the time with connected graphs. However, graphs need not be connected in general.

Directed graph terminology

If there is a directed edge from vertex v_1 to v_2, v_1 is said to be *adjacent to* v_2, or alternatively v_2 is *adjacent from* v_1. In G_2 (Figure 3.2), A is adjacent to D and E is adjacent from D. A (directed) path is a tuple of vertices $(v_1, v_2, \cdots, v_n)$, such that v_1 is adjacent to v_2 and v_2 is adjacent to v_3 and so on. A (directed) path is called a (directed) *cycle* or *circuit* if $v_1 = v_n$. In G_2, the path (B, C, A, D, E, A, B) is a circuit. The *in-degree* of a vertex is the number of vertices that are adjacent to it and the *out-degree* is the number of vertices that are adjacent from it. In G_2, A has an in-degree of 3 (3 arrows are coming in) and out-degree of 2 (2 arrows are going out).

Multigraphs

The definition of graphs (directed or undirected) does not allow multiple edges between any pair of vertices. In the set E_G of some graph G, the edge (u, v) or $\{u, v\}$ can only occur once (recall that sets count repeated elements only once). However for some applications, it is sometimes unavoidable to have multiple edges between vertices. A graph that allows multiple edges between a pair of vertices is called a *multigraph*. The set of edges in a multigraph is a multiset. Recall that unlike sets, multisets allow the repetition of elements.

Example 3.4

The World Wide Web can be modeled as a directed multigraph. The vertices are the Web pages, and the edges are the hyperlinks. A Web page may have several hyperlinks to another Web page.

3.2   Euler Paths

The town of Kaliningrad in the Russian Republic used to be called Konigsberg in the 18th century and it was part of Prussia at that time. The Pregel River passes through Konigsberg, creating a nice layout with seven bridges, as shown in Figure 3.4. In Figure 3.4, land is marked with A (island), B, C, and D. Sometime in the 18th century, the people of Konigsberg wondered if there was a tour that started somewhere in town, crossing all bridges, crossing each bridge exactly once, and ending up where the tour started. Since they could not figure out whether or not such a tour was possible, they wrote to the famous Swiss mathematician Leonhard Euler seeking help. Euler came up with general theorems that identify the conditions, under which a graph has such a circuit. Since the Konigsberg layout can be represented as a multigraph, his theorem can be used to answer the Konigsberg question. The vertices in the Konigsberg graph (Figure 3.5) are the land bodies and the edges are simply the bridges. Therefore, the problem is reduced to finding a circuit crossing all edges and crossing each edge once. Such a circuit is called an *Euler circuit*.

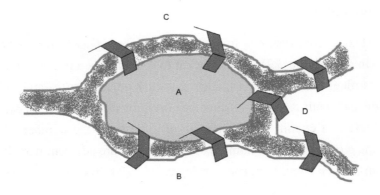

Figure 3.4: Konigsberg town layout

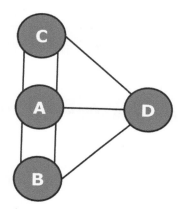

Figure 3.5: Konigsberg multigraph

Since multigraphs are more general than graphs (graphs are special cases of multigraphs), Euler's observations for multigraphs also apply to graphs.

Euler's theorem states that an undirected multigraph has an Euler circuit *if and only if* all of its vertices have even degrees. That is, Euler's theorem can be stated in predicate logic as follows. Given a particular undirected multigraph $G = (V_G, E_G)$, [has-Euler-circuit$(G) \rightarrow \forall v \in V_G$, even-degree$(v)$] $\wedge$ [$\forall v \in V_G$, even-degree$(v) \rightarrow$ has-Euler-circuit(G)].

An informal argument to Euler's theorem follows. If a multigraph has at least one vertex with an odd degree, then an Euler circuit does not exist for this multigraph. Such an odd vertex, call it O, cannot be the starting and ending point of the tour. To start from O, an edge must be used to leave and a different edge must be used to end the tour at O. So, O has to have a degree of at least 2, which is not odd. Well, what if during the tour, you come back to O to leave again before the tour ends? In such a case, every time you visit O, you must come in using a new edge (never used before), and you must leave using another new edge. Hence, each such visit uses 2 edges, leaving us with an even degree for the start vertex. Therefore, the vertex O cannot be the start/end vertex.

Furthermore, O and cannot be any other vertex. Any other vertex would also have an even degree because you always visit this vertex using a new edge (O is not the start vertex) and you must leave it using another new edge (O is not the end vertex). No matter how many times you visit the vertex, each time you're using 2 edges and the degree of this vertex must be even, if you do not want to leave uncrossed edges behind.

Given an undirected multigraph G where all vertices have even degrees, the algorithm Euler_Circuit(G) constructs an Euler circuit for G.

Algorithm 3.1. — *Euler_Circuit(G) algorithm* _____

Input: *G, an undirected multigraph, where all vertices have even degrees*

Output: *Euler circuit for G*

1. *Construct a circuit, starting and ending at an arbitrary vertex in G, call this circuit c*

2. *Remove the edges used in c from G*

3. *Repeat the following until G has no edges*

    (a) *Construct a circuit in G that starts (ends) in a vertex v that is in c, call this circuit c′*

    (b) *Add c′ into c at v*

    (c) *Remove the edges of c′ from G*

Example 3.5 _____

Consider the graph G of Figure 3.6(a). Each vertex of G has an even degree, so an Euler circuit exists for G.

Step 1 of Algorithm 3.1 tells us to find a circuit starting at an arbitrary vertex. One such circuit is: (A, B, D, C, A). The edges of this circuit are $\{A, B\}$, $\{B, D\}$, $\{D, C\}$, and $\{C, A\}$. Other possible circuits may also be used as a starting point.

In step 2, all the edges of the circuit (A, B, D, C, A) are removed from G. This is shown in Figure 3.6(b). Note that this results in a graph that is not connected.

Since we still have edges in G, we apply steps 3a to 3c. Step 3a can result in the following circuit (A, I, J, A). Note that such a circuit must start at a vertex that is part of the circuit constructed in step 1. We choose vertex A. Vertex D could have been another choice. Adding (A, I, J, A) to (A, B, D, C, A) results in the circuit: (A, I, J, A, B, D, C, A). (We could have also added (A, I, J, A) at the second occurrence of A in (A, B, D, C, A), resulting in (A, B, D, C, A, I, J, A)). Deleting the edges $\{A, I\}$, $\{I, J\}$, and $\{A, J\}$ from G, yields the graph of Figure 3.6(c). G still has edges and step 3a results in the circuit (D, F, E, D). Adding this circuit to (A, I, J, A, B, D, C, A) results in: $(A, I, J, A, B, D, F, E, D, C, A)$, which is an Euler circuit as required. Deleting the edges $\{D, F\}$, $\{F, E\}$, and $\{E, D\}$ from G leaves G with no edges (Figure 3.6(d)). Therefore, the algorithm terminates.

A simpler version of the Konigsberg problem is to find an Euler *path*. Such a path still needs to cross every edge once, but can start and end in different vertices. Euler noticed that a graph G has an Euler path if and only if G has only two vertices with odd degrees. These are the starting and ending vertices of the Euler path.

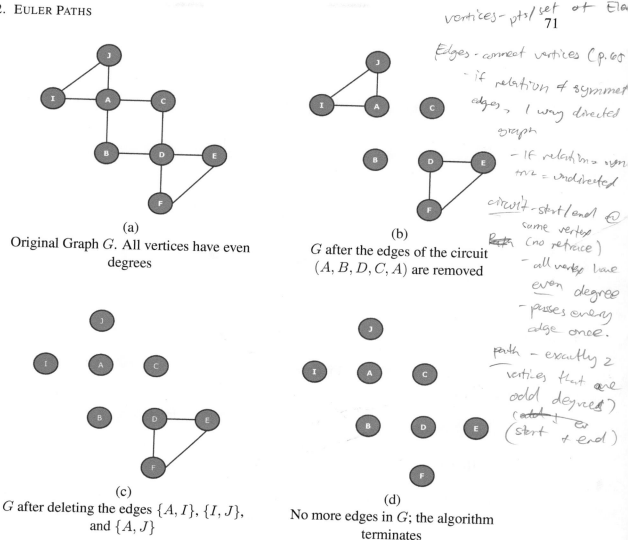

(a)

Original Graph G. All vertices have even
degrees

(b)

G after the edges of the circuit
(A, B, D, C, A) are removed

(c)

G after deleting the edges $\{A, I\}, \{I, J\}$,
and $\{A, J\}$

(d)

No more edges in G; the algorithm
terminates

Figure 3.6: Constructing an Euler tour

Edges - connect vertices (p. 65
- if relation ≠ symmet
edges, 1 way directed
graph
- if relation≠ sym
tve = undirected
circuit - start/end @
same vertex
(no retrace)
- all verts have
even degree
- passes every
edge once.
path - exactly 2
vertices that are
odd degrees)
(start + end)

Example 3.6

Can you draw an envelope shape (Figure 3.7) using the following rules?

- Draw in continuous motion; you cannot lift the pen and move it from one position
  to another.

- Draw so that no line is retraced; you cannot let the pen run on top of an already
  drawn line.

The problem is reduced to finding an Euler path in the graph shown in Figure 3.8.

This graph has two vertices with odd degrees, namely D and E. So any Euler path must
start at one and end at the other. That is, you can draw this shape if you start at D and
stop at E or vice versa. One such path is $(D, B, E, C, A, B, C, D, E)$.

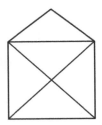

Figure 3.7: Envelope shape

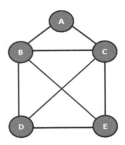

Figure 3.8: Envelope graph

3.3 Graph Coloring

Graph coloring works on an undirected graph and produces a coloring of the vertices of the input graph, such that no two adjacent vertices have the same color and the number of colors used is nearly minimized.

One idea might be to color each vertex with a different color; however, this violates the specification of the problem, requiring that the number of colors be nearly minimized. This is especially desirable for larger graphs. However, in some graphs, the minimum number of colors is equal to the number of vertices. Can you think of such a graph?

Graph coloring is very useful when solving scheduling problems, such as making sure that no two courses with the same time can be scheduled in the same class room.

Example 3.7

Figure 3.9 shows a possible coloring for graph G_1 (Figure 3.1). Note that 3 colors is the minimum number of colors that can be used for this graph.

So how do we transform the input into the required output? This is the job of the Graph_Coloring(G) algorithm, where G is an undirected graph.

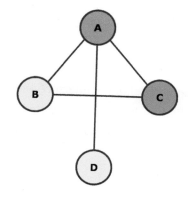

Figure 3.9: Coloring of graph G_1

Algorithm 3.2. — *Graph_Coloring(G) algorithm* _____
Input: *an undirected graph, G*
Output: *colored G*
Repeat the following two steps until all the vertices in G are colored:

1. *Select an uncolored vertex in G and color it with a new color:* **c**

2. *For each uncolored vertex v in G,*

   - *If v is adjacent to a vertex that is already colored with color **c**, skip v*

   - *Otherwise, color v with color **c***

_____

As mentioned earlier, graph coloring can be very useful in solving scheduling problems. The items that need to be scheduled are arranged into a graph as vertices, and the edges indicate which items are conflicting and cannot be scheduled at the same time. Coloring the graph allows us to group the items so that the ones in the same group (ones with the same color) can be scheduled at the same time.

Note that Algorithm 3.2 does not specify a strict order in which vertices are considered. For instance, in an initially uncolored graph, any vertex can be chosen in step 1. In addition, the uncolored vertices in step 2, can be considered in any order. This can produce different colorings of the same input graph.

Example 3.8 _____

Consider the traffic intersection in Figure 3.10. The objective is to determine which traffic flows can run simultaneously. Intersections are an expensive resource, and maximizing their use is desirable. Thus, the naive solution of letting traffic flow only in one direction is undesirable; after all, we do not do this in real life. For instance, traffic from A to D (denoted by AD), A to C (denoted by AC), and B to A (denoted by BA) can all run simultaneously.

This is a scheduling problem, and we can use graph coloring to determine the groups of traffic flows that are non-conflicting. Since the graph coloring algorithm minimizes the number of colors used, it maximizes the traffic flow.

Figure 3.11 shows a graph model of the intersection where each vertex represents a traffic flow direction, and conflicting flows are connected by edges. The graph is also colored using the graph coloring algorithm, showing three groups (colors) of traffic flows.

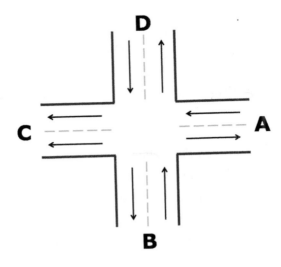

Figure 3.10: Traffic intersection

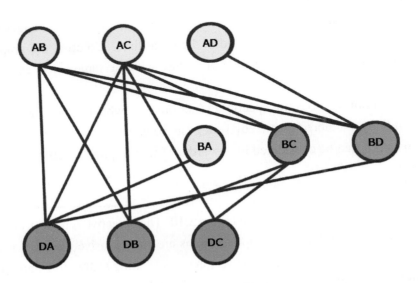

Figure 3.11: Traffic intersection graph

3.4 Trees

Trees are a special case of graphs. A *tree* is a directed graph that has the following two properties:

1. There is a designated vertex called the *root* of the tree, and

2. There is a unique directed path from the root to every other vertex in the tree

These properties ensure that the in-degree of the root is 0, and the in-degree of any other vertex is 1.

Example 3.9

A tree is drawn downwards with the root on the top. The root of the tree T of Figure 3.12 is A. Often, we drop the arrows, since it is always understood that the edges direction is downwards. The trees of figures 3.12 and 3.13 are the same.

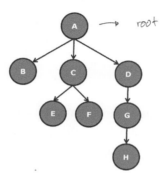

Figure 3.12: Tree T

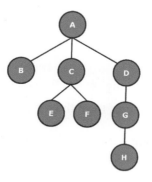

Figure 3.13: Tree T with undirected edges

Example 3.10

In games, trees are used to explore all possibilities of a game. The root is the start of the game, and the path from the root to a leaf explores one possible outcome of the game. In the game tree of Figure 3.14, **1S** indicates that player 1 chooses scissors; **1R** indicates that player 1 chooses rock; and **1P** is player 1's choice of paper. The notation is similar for player 2. Each path from the root to a leaf captures one possible instance of the game.

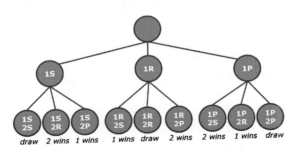

Figure 3.14: Tree for the paper-scissors-rock game

For other more complex games, such as chess, the tree can become prohibitively large.

Tree terminology

A vertex which is adjacent from some vertex v, is call a *child* of v. In tree T (Figure 3.13), E and F are children of C. If a vertex v is a child of vertex w, then w is the *parent* of v. All vertices have exactly one parent, except the root which does not have a parent. A vertex that does not have any children is called a *leaf*. In tree T, the vertices B, E, F and H are leaves. The *distance* of a vertex v from the root is the number of edges on the path from the root to v. In tree T, B is at distance 1 from the root, and H is at distance 3 from the root. Finally, a collection of trees is called a *forest*.

Binary trees

A *binary tree* is a tree that has the following two additional properties:

1. The edges are labeled with the labels from the set {*left*, *right*}, and

2. Every vertex has at most two children; if both children exist, then one edge must be labeled *left* and the other *right*.

Example 3.11

An example binary tree is shown in Figure 3.15. Just as we have dropped the arrows, we can also drop the labels, if we always draw the tree in such a way that left children are drawn on our left and the right ones on our right. The binary tree T of Figure 3.15 can be drawn as in Figure 3.16, without any confusion about who's who in the left and right world.

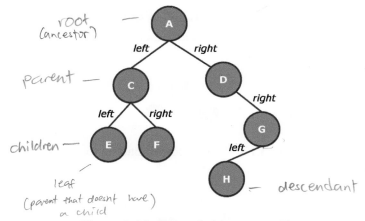

Figure 3.15: Example binary tree T

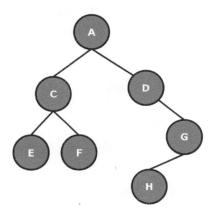

Figure 3.16: The binary tree T without edge labels

BL-Trees

Some binary trees make no distinction between the names (or labels) of non-leaf vertices, such as the tree depicted in Figure 3.18. We use the term *BL-tree* to refer to such a binary tree. That is, in a BL-tree, only the leaves contain application data.

There are different ways by which trees are represented in a computer. Since trees are graphs, we can use adjacency matrices. However, this is not the best way. We will only discuss representing BL-trees here. A BL-tree can be represented as a nested or recursive list or tuple.

The representation is recursive. The basis case is when we have a tree of one vertex, often called a *degenerate* tree. In such a case, the root is a leaf, and the tree is represented by the value stored in this leaf. For example, A represents the tree: Ⓐ. The recursive case, defines a BL-tree as a list of two subtrees: [left-subtree, right-subtree]. The list $[1, 2]$ represents the tree of Figure 3.17. Any of the left-subtree or right-subtree can be a list by itself representing a subtree. For instance the list $[1, [2, 3]]$ has 1 as a left child and $[2, 3]$ as a right child, which is itself a tree. The tree is shown in Figure 3.18. Any of the elements 1,2, or 3 can be replaced by a list of size 2 and so on. This allows us to create complex trees such as the one in Figure 3.19, corresponding to the list $[f, [[[e, d], [c, a]], b]]$.

Figure 3.17: BL-tree corresponding to $[1, 2]$

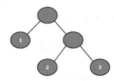

Figure 3.18: BL-tree corresponding to $[1, [2, 3]]$

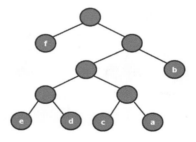

Figure 3.19: BL-tree corresponding to $[f, [[[e, d], [c, a]], b]]$

3.5   Variable-length Coding

In Chapter 1, we saw how information in a computer is always coded with 0s and 1s. For instance, we saw how characters can be given fixed-length codes of 0s and 1s, such as in ASCII coding. Coding of a set of symbols S is solved by finding a coding function that assigns to each symbol in S a unique binary code. The code assigned to symbol α of S is denoted by CODE(α).

Example 3.12
_____

Assume that we have a file containing information formed from 6 distinct characters only: A, I, C, D, E, and S. If such a file has 1000 characters in total, how many bits are needed to code the file? First, we need to determine the length of the codes. One attempt is to use codes of length 2, but this is not enough. This would only allow us to represent 4 distinct characters, since $2^2 = 4$. Since $2^3 = 8$, 3 bits is more than enough because we have only 6 distinct characters. Therefore, the file would require $3 \times 1000 = 3000$ bits.

An interesting question is whether the size of a text file we can be reduced or compressed. One idea is that if some characters are more frequent than others, we should give them shorter codes than the less frequent ones. This gives rise to *variable-length* codes.

Example 3.13

Assume that we have analyzed the file of Example 3.12 and found the following statistics: 35% of the characters in the file is S; 28% is A; 20% is E; 7% is I; 6% is C; and 4% is D.

We can use 2 bits to represent each of S, E, and A (the most frequent ones), 3 bits to represent I and 4 bits for each of C and D.

If we use this coding, what is the size of the file? 350 S's (35% of 1000) require 700 bits (2 bits for each S); 200 E's require 400 bits; 280 A's require 560 bits; 70 I's require 210 bits; 60 C's require 240 bits; 40 D's require 160 bits. The total is 2270 bits. Recall that with fixed-length codes, the size is 3000 bits. The compressed file size is about 76% of the original file size.

Not all variable-length coding schemes work. Assume CODE(A)= 0, CODE(C)= 1, and CODE(E) = 01. The code 0101 could correspond to *ACE*, *EAC*, *ACAC*, or *EE*. A coding that works must have the property that each code has a unique interpretation. Variable-length codes that have unique interpretations must have the property that no code can be the prefix of another code. These are called *non-prefix* codes. 0 is a prefix of 01, and this is why our example coding failed.

Non-prefix codes can be generated using a BL-tree. We interpret a *left* label as 0 and the *right* label as 1. Each path from the root of the tree to a leaf represents a code, and all these codes are non-prefix codes.

Example 3.14

The BL-tree of Figure 3.20 has the symbols A, B, C, D, E, and F stored in the leaves. The left labels are replaced with 0s and the right labels with 1s. The labels on the path from the root to the leaves result in the following non-prefix codes: CODE(A)=00, CODE(B)=0100, CODE(C)=0101, CODE(D)=011, CODE(E)=10, and CODE(F)=11.

The code 111010011 represents the word *FEED*, and there is no confusion about that.

So how do we generate non-prefix, variable-length codes such that the most frequent characters have shorter codes than the less frequent characters? Huffman's algorithm allows us to do just this. The input of this algorithm is a list of symbols and their frequencies, and the output is non-prefix, variable-length codes for each input symbol, such that the characters with higher frequencies have shorter codes, where possible. *Huffman's algorithm* arranges the input symbols into a BL-tree, ensuring that the more frequent characters have shorter distances from the root. Let S

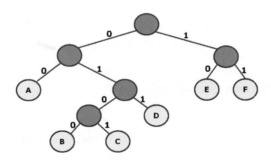

Figure 3.20: Generating non-prefix codes from a binary tree

be a set of pairs, each consisting of a symbol and its weight (or frequency). In Example 3.13, $S = \{(A, 28), (C, 6), (D, 4), (E, 20), (S, 35), (I, 7)\}$.

Algorithm 3.3. — *Huffman(S) algorithm* _____

Input: *S, a set of symbol-weight pairs*

Output: *binary tree*

1. *For each pair $(a, b) \in S$, build a tree t with one vertex a only. Let $w(t) = b$. Call the resulting forest F.*

2. *Repeat the following until F consists of a single tree:*

    (a) *Choose two trees t and t' such that $w(t)$ and $w(t')$ are minimum*

    (b) *Replace t and t' by a new tree n with new root r*

    (c) *If $w(t) \leq w(t')$, t is the right child of r; otherwise, t is the left child of r*

    (d) *Assign tree n the weight $w(n) = w(t) + w(t')$*

3. *Interpret the* left *labels as 0s and the* right *labels as 1s. Assign each leaf the code consisting of the labels of the edges on the path from the root to that leaf.*

Example 3.15 _____

Consider the symbols and their frequencies of Example 3.13. The input to Huffman's algorithms is $\{(A, 28), (C, 6), (D, 4), (E, 20), (S, 35), (I, 7)\}$.

Step 1 generates the forest F:

Since F consists of more than one tree, step 2 is applied. The trees with minimum weights are D and C with $w(D) = 4$ and $w(C) = 6$. These trees are combined into a single tree $[C, D]$ with weight 10. The resulting forest F is:

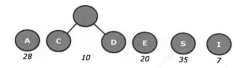

Applying step 2 again results in choosing the trees I and $[C, D]$, with $w(I) = 7$ and $w([C, D]) = 10$. They are combined into a new tree $[[C, D], I]$ with weight 17:

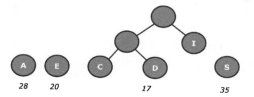

Applying step 2 again results in choosing the trees $[[C, D], I]$ and E. They are combined into a new tree $[E, [[C, D], I]]$ with weight 37:

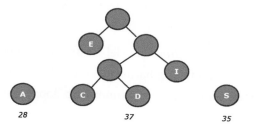

Applying step 2 again results in choosing the trees A and S, with $w(A) = 28$ and $w(S) = 35$. They are combined into a new tree $[S, A]$ with weight 63:

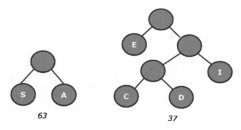

Applying step 2 for the last time results in a single tree $[[S, A], [E, [[C, D], I]]]$ in F:

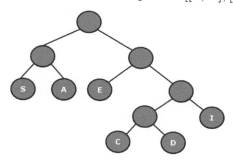

Finally the codes are assigned as in the following tree:

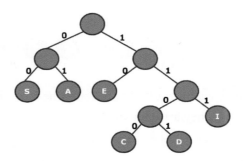

That is, CODE(S)=00, CODE(A)=01, CODE(E)=10, CODE(C)=1100, CODE(D)=1101, and CODE(I)=111.

3.6   Finite State Machines

A *finite state machine* (abbreviated FSM) is a special kind of a directed graph with two properties:

1. The set of vertices, called *states*, is finite, and

2. The edges are *labeled transitions* (the labels are also called *events*).

FSMs are very handy when designing hardware controllers, such as the ones found in remote controls, traffic lights, vending machines, and automatic doors. An example FSM is given in Figure 3.21. This FSM has two states: *hungry* and *full* and two events: *eat* and *jog*. The directed edges are labeled with events that trigger transitions from one state to another. So, if you are in the *hungry* state and you jog, you will still be *hungry*. However, if you eat, the state changes to *full*. Eating while you're *full* does not change the fact that you're *full*, but jogging will make you *hungry* again.

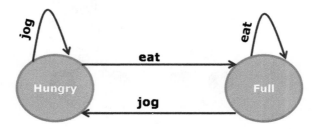

Figure 3.21: A simple FSM

Consider an automatic sliding door that opens when people step on its front or rear pads (Figure 3.22). An FSM that controls the door is given in Figure 3.23. The door can be in one of two states: OPEN or CLOSED. The events that can occur are:

FRONT: someone steps on the front pad

REAR: someone steps on the read pad

BOTH: both pads have someone stepping on them

NONE: neither pad has someone stepping on it

We allow an edge to have more than one label. So, if the door is CLOSED and any of the events FRONT, REAR, or BOTH takes place, the door should OPEN. It only goes back to the CLOSED state in the case of the NONE event.

The graphical representation of an FSM as a graph is called a *state diagram*. We can also represent the FSM as a matrix, called *state table*. We choose to represent it in the way shown in Table 3.1 (there are shorter forms of state table representations).

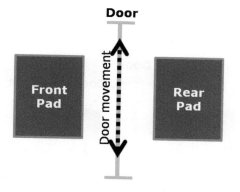

Figure 3.22: An automatic sliding door

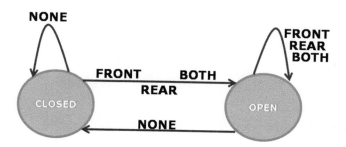

Figure 3.23: An FSM for an automatic sliding controller

Input	Current State	Next State
NONE	CLOSED	CLOSED
NONE	OPEN	CLOSED
FRONT	CLOSED	OPEN
FRONT	OPEN	OPEN
REAR	CLOSED	OPEN
REAR	OPEN	OPEN
BOTH	CLOSED	OPEN
BOTH	OPEN	OPEN

Table 3.1: A state table for an automatic sliding controller

Example 3.17

Consider an automatic door that opens both ways toward the pads (Figure 3.24). An FSM that controls the door is given in Figure 3.25 and the state table in Table 3.2. In this version, we have to split the OPEN state to two: OPENR, open to the rear, and OPENF, open to the front. This is necessary because if someone steps on the front pad (respectively, rear pad) it will be unsafe to open the door to the front (respectively, the rear).

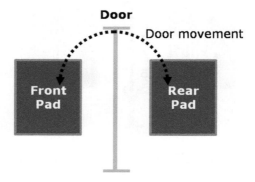

Figure 3.24: A two-way automatic door

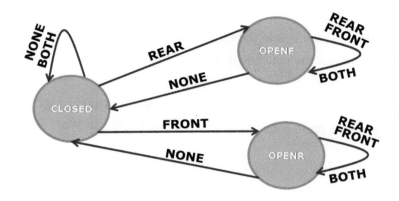

Figure 3.25: An FSM for a two-way automatic door controller

Input	Current State	Next State
NONE	CLOSED	CLOSED
NONE	OPENF	CLOSED
NONE	OPENR	CLOSED
FRONT	OPENF	OPENF
FRONT	CLOSED	OPENR
FRONT	OPENR	OPENR
REAR	CLOSED	OPENF
REAR	OPENF	OPENF
REAR	OPENR	OPENR
BOTH	CLOSED	CLOSED
BOTH	OPENF	OPENF
BOTH	OPENR	OPENR

Table 3.2: A state table for a two-way automatic door controller

Example 3.18

A simple vending machine (Figure 3.26) dispenses $3 phone cards. It accepts $1 and $2 coins only. It does not give any change. If the user exceeds the $3 amount, the machine gives the money back without dispensing any phone cards. It can dispense one phone card at a time. The machine has two buttons: CANCEL to cancel the transaction and COLLECT to dispense the phone card. The machine keeps the collected coins in a coin collector until a card is dispensed, in which case the coins are dropped into the piggy bank and cannot be recovered by the user.

An FSM that controls the vending machine requires five states:

ONE: the total amount in the coin collector is $1

TWO: the total amount in the coin collector is $2

THREE: the total amount in the coin collector is $3

ZERO: the total amount in the coin collector is $0. This is the initial state of the machine. When the machine is turned on it starts in this state. The machine goes to this state when the user presses CANCEL

DISP: this is the state when the machine dispenses a card, drops in the coins into the piggy bank (coin collector becomes empty), and gets ready for the next user

The events are:

$1: the user inserts a $1 coin

$2: the user inserts a $2 coin

CANCEL: the user presses CANCEL

COLLECT: the user presses COLLECT

The FSM is give in Figure 3.27.

Figure 3.26: A simple vending machine

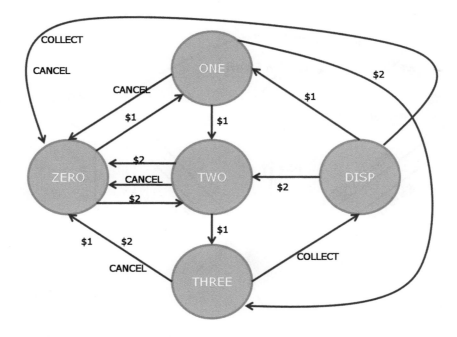

Figure 3.27: An FSM for the simple vending machine

Example 3.19

An FSM for the wall-hugging robot of Chapter 1 is given in Figure 3.28. Note that in this FSM, we are allowing transition labels to be logical expressions. This allows us to represent the FSM in a more concise way.

The FSM states are:

ON: the robot has just been turned on

FW?: the robot takes a step (forward) searching for a wall

F: the robot is hugging the wall, it takes a step (forward)

L: the robot turns left (in the same square)

R: the robot turns right (in the same square)

(We can add an OFF state, which is reached by switching the power button off, from any state. This is straightforward and is left out.)

The transitions are:

RS=S: the right sensor senses space

RS=w: the right sensor senses a wall

FS=S: the front sensor senses space

FS=w: the front sensor senses a wall

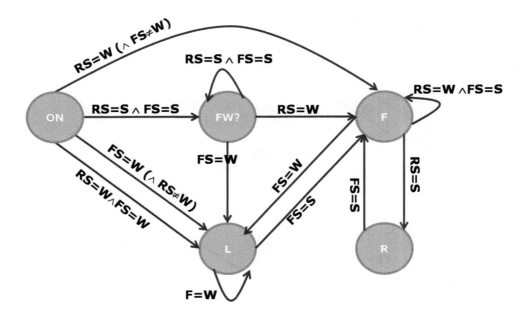

Figure 3.28: An FSM for the wall-hugging robot

Exercises

1. Construct an algorithm that inputs an adjacency matrix and checks if the matrix is symmetric or not.

2. Describe how an unlabeled multigraph can be represented using an adjacency matrix. What if the multigraph is labeled?

3. Modify Euler's circuit algorithm so that it finds an Euler's path, not necessarily a circuit.

4. According to Euler's theorem, a graph that does not have any edges has an Euler circuit, since all vertices, if any, have a degree of 0, which is even. What is the Euler circuit of such a graph?

5. Identify problems that can be solved by graph coloring.

6. Construct an example graph consisting of at least 5 vertices, such that the minimum number of colors required for the graph is equal to the number of vertices.

7. Give an example of a graph with more than one vertex that can be colored by one color only.

8. Political maps are colored in such a way that no two countries that share a border can have the same color. Formulate this problem as a graph coloring problem.

9. Suggest an algorithm that counts the number of vertices in a binary tree.

10. Suggest an algorithm that counts the number of leaf vertices in a binary tree.

11. Draw the tree represented by the recursive list $[[[x, [[y, h], h]], e], [n, [k, [r, c]]]]$.

12. How many bits are required to code 8 characters A to H using fixed-length codes. Choose the shortest possible codes.

13. If a file contains 10000 characters from the characters (A to H), how many bits will the size of the file be, using your coding from the previous question?

14. Apply Huffman's algorithm to the following input: $(A, 23\%)$, $(B, 60\%)$, $(C, 4\%)$, $(D, 3\%)$, $(E, 2\%)$, $(F, 2\%)$, $(G, 5\%)$, $(H, 1\%)$. Generate variable-length codes for the characters A to H.

15. Repeat question 13, using the codes from question 14. What is the percentage of savings compared to the file size from question 13?

16. Design an FSM for a garage door controller. Garage doors receive signals from a remote control with one button. If the button is pressed, the door opens when it is closed and vice versa. If the button is pressed while the door is in motion, the door stops; when the button is pressed again, the door starts moving but it reverses the direction it was going before it was stopped.

17. Modify the vending machine FSM to allow the machine to accept two $2 coins and return a $1 coin back.

18. Design an FSM for a similar vending machine that has two types of cards: $3 and $4 cards. The machine would have two COLLECT buttons to choose one for each type of card. The machine also gives $1 change.

19. Modify the wall-hugging robot's FSM, assuming the robot can only turn right.

CHAPTER 4

Working with Large Data: Databases

Computer programs process data. When the amount of data becomes large, data organization becomes crucial. We all organize our data, from shopping lists to budget records. Nevertheless, large amounts of data need to be carefully designed and organized. The simple list structure of "to-do" lists falls short for larger data sets. Banks keep information about all their customers, accounts, and even all the transactions performed on each account. This is a lot of data that needs to be organized so that the computer programs work properly on bank data.

A *database* is an organized collection of data. Your mobile phone uses a database to store your address book. The university uses a database to keep track of students, their course and grades, and much more. In this chapter, we will learn how to design data models. Such models, if properly designed, lead to properly designed databases. Once we learn how to model data and design databases, we will look at a programming language, called SQL, that is meant to interact with databases.

4.1 Relational Databases

A *database* organizes related data so that it is easy to use, and it minimizes redundancy. Redundancy not only wastes space but can also lead to undesired anomalies, as we shall see later in this chapter. The most common way to organize structured data is a *relational database*.

A relational database is a collection of *tables*. An example database for keeping the records of a simple company is given in Figure 4.1. We will use this database as a running example throughout the chapter.

The PROJECT table can be represented in set notation as follows:

PROJECT $= \{(1, \textit{Web Shopping}, \textit{Calgary}, 1), (2, \textit{Backup}, \textit{Calgary}, 1),$
$\qquad (3, \textit{New benefits}, \textit{Toronto}, 2), (4, \textit{XT345}, \textit{Toronto}, 3)\}.$

A table is a set of tuples. Database experts call each row in a table a *tuple* and each table a *relation*. It should be easily seen if:

EMPLOYEE

SIN	Fname	Lname	DOB	Gender	Salary	Snumber	Street	City	Pcode	Dnumber
171717171	Debra	Beacon	15-Aug-1961	Female	70000	15	Baron Hill	Calgary	T2X Y0Y	1
181817178	Sam	Field	17-Feb-1978	Male	40000	15	Kick Way	Calgary	Y2K K0K	1
123456789	Rajeet	Folk	30-Apr-1967	Male	78000	123	One Road	Toronto	H1H J9J	2
987654321	Marie	Band	12-Jan-1985	Female	53500	2828	Exit Close	Toronto	K8O O8K	2
666333999	Saleh	Dice	25-Mar-1970	Male	90400	66	Straight Way	Toronto	T4E T6B	3

DEPARTMENT

Dnumber	Dname	MGR_SIN	StartDate
1	IT	171717171	12-Feb-2008
2	Finance	123456789	1-Mar-2002
3	Marketing	666333999	1-Jan-2005

PROJECT

Pnumber	Pname	Location	Dnumber
1	Web Shopping	Calgary	1
2	Network Upgrade	Calgary	1
3	New Benefits	Toronto	2
4	Product XT345	Toronto	3

PROJ_EMP

SIN	Pnumber	Hours
171717171	1	15
171717171	2	20
171717171	4	5
181817178	1	30
181817178	2	10
123456789	3	40
666333999	4	40

Figure 4.1: A sample relational database containing records of a simple company

N is the set of natural numbers,

M is the set of names, and

L is the set of locations, then

PROJECT $\subseteq N \times M \times L \times N$.

In other words, PROJECT is a relation on the sets: N, M, L, and N.

The tables of Figure 4.1 are not independent of one another; the are related by *relationships* (not to be confused with *relations*). The Dnumber *column* or *attribute* of EMPLOYEE tells us the *department number* an employee works for. For instance, employee *Sam Field* works for the department whose number is 1. The DEPARTMENT relation indicates that this is the *IT* department. Similarly, *Rajeet Folk* works for the department whose number is 2, which is the *Finance* department.

There are more relationships in Figure 4.1. Try to identify and understand them.

EMPLOYEE

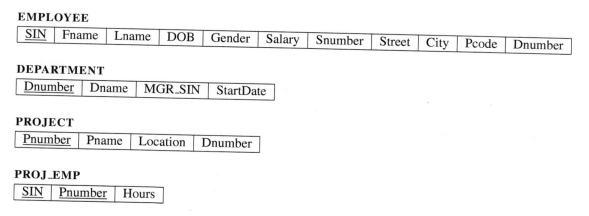

DEPARTMENT

PROJECT

PROJ_EMP

Figure 4.2: The schema for the database of Figure 4.1

In reality, databases can be very large, and it may not be possible to give a snapshot of the database as we have done in Figure 4.1. Instead, a *database schema* is always available, which defines the columns of the relations. Figure 4.2 gives the schema for the database of Figure 4.1.

4.2 Data Modeling

Before a database is created, a *data model* must be first defined. A data model is simply a specification of the data that needs to be kept in the database.

The data modeling approach we discuss in this chapter is called the *Entity-Relationship model*, abbreviated ER. Data can be modeled as *entities* and *relationships* between these entities.

Entities and entity-types

An *entity* is any object that exists in the real world. Such an object can exist physically, in a tangible way, or conceptually, in a virtual way. A book, car, student, and jacket are all examples of physical entities. A course, bus route, and job are entities of conceptual existence. An *entity-type* specifies a class of entities. The employee *Sam Field* is an entity of type employee; so is *Saleh Dice*. These entities are of the same type: employee. All employees share common characteristics. An entity-type defines these common characteristics. For instance, all employees have names; this is a common characteristic. Two different employees may have different names, but they have to have names. Another common characteristic is the salary; all employees earn a salary. The value of the salary could be different between employees.

Typical entity-types in a company, such as our simple company example, include EMPLOYEE, PROJECT, and DEPARTMENT.

Attributes

Entities have attributes, properties that describe them. An employee for instance can be described by a name, date of birth, salary, address, etc. The choice of the attributes is determined by the problem we are trying to solve. These attributes will be assigned values, which could be different from one entity to another. A collection of attributes that uniquely identify an entity is called a *primary key*.

ER diagrams and entity-types

An ER model is specified as a diagram, called an ERD, which is a labeled undirected multigraph. There are two types of vertices in this multigraph. The first type of vertices is the entity-types. These vertices are drawn as boxes (Figure 4.3). The attributes of each entity-type are listed inside its corresponding box in the ERD.

An employee can be described by the attributes: social insurance number (SIN), name (first and last), date of birth (DOB), gender, salary, and address (street number, street, city, and postal code). A department has a number and a name. In addition, a project has a location.

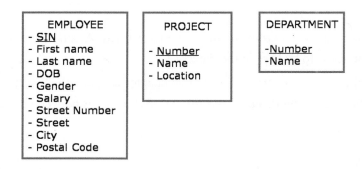

Figure 4.3: Entity-types of the simple company

The attribute SIN of EMPLOYEE is underlined to indicate that it is a primary key for EMPLOYEE. No two employees can have the same SIN. Similarly, Number in PROJECT is the primary key. The department Number is the primary key for DEPARTMENT.

Take a specific entity of EMPLOYEE, *Debra Beacon*. It may have the following values assigned to its attributes: (171717171, *Debra*, *Beacon*, *15-Aug-1961*, *Female*, $70,000, 15, *Baron Hill*, *Calgary*, *T2X Y0Y*). Similarly, entity *Sam Field* can be described by: (181817178, *Sam*, *Field*, 17-Feb-1978, *Male*, $40,000, 15, *Kick Way*, *Calgary*, *Y2K K0K*).

This ERD of Figure 4.3 is not complete yet. It does not contain relationship information (the R of ER). How does an employee relate to a department? How do employees relate to projects?

Relationships and relationship-types

A *relationship-type* specifies how entity-types relate to one another. A *relationship* is an instance of the relationship-type. Relationship-types are the second kind of vertices in the ERD multigraph. These vertices are drawn as diamond shapes. An edge always connects an entity-type vertex to a relationship-type vertex.

Figure 4.4 shows the ERD after adding the edges. EMPLOYEE and DEPARTMENT are related by the relationship-type WORKS FOR, which captures which employee works for which department. EMPLOYEE and PROJECT are related by WORKS ON, capturing which projects an employee is working on. Finally, CONTROLS relates DEPARTMENT and PROJECT, allowing us to keep track of which projects are controlled by which department.

Cardinality of relationship-types

An important piece of extra information needed for the ERD is the *cardinality* of the relationship-types. There are three cardinality types:

- **One-to-one:** This cardinality represents a unique association between entities.

- **One-to-many (many-to-one):** An entity can be associated with more than one other entity. A department can have many employees, but an employee is allowed to belong to only one department.

- **Many-to-many:** This cardinality associates many entities with many other entities. An employee can work on more than one project, and a project may have several employees working on it.

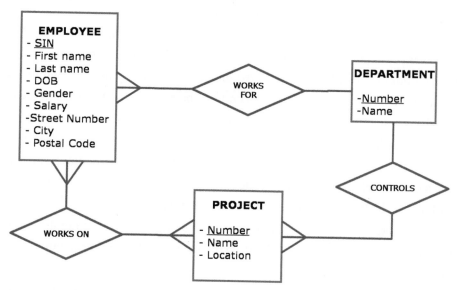

Figure 4.4: ERD of the simple company

The cardinalities of the relationship-types of Figure 4.4 are indicated pictorially. For instance, WORKS FOR is a one-to-many relationship-type: one department can have *many* employees, indicated by the *forking* edge ($\succ$) when touching EMPLOYEE, but an employee can be in *one* department only, indicated by a *non-forking* edge (__) when touching DEPARTMENT.

The relationship-type CONTROLS is also one-to-many. A department can control *many* projects, but a project must be controlled by *one* department only. Note that this model does not allow inter-departmental projects, or at least it delegates the project control to a single department. Had inter-departmental projects been allowed, CONTROLS would have been a many-to-many relationship-type, and the edge at the DEPARTMENT end would have been a forking edge.

Finally, WORKS ON is many-to-many: many employees can be working on the same project, and an employee is allowed to work on more than one project at the same time. The WORKS ON edges fork on both entity-type ends.

Relationship-type degrees

The *degree* of a relationship-type is the number of entity-types it relates. WORKS ON, WORKS FOR, and CONTROLS are all *binary* (of degree 2) relationship-types. Each relates two entity-types. Relationship-types could be of any degree, relating as many entity-types as needed. Relationship types of very high degrees seldom occur in practice. In this book, we limit the discussion to binary relationship-types.

Participation levels

It is often helpful to include further information on the edges of the ERD, such as how each entity participates in the relationship. Does every employee have to work on a project? Does every department control some project? There are two levels of participation in a relationship, *universal* or *full*, and *existential* or *partial*. These are also indicated pictorially as is shown in Figure 4.5. A *dotted* edge to an entity-type indicates that this entity-type partially participates in the relationship-type. A *solid* edge to an entity-type indicates its full participation in the relationship-type.

The EMPLOYEE side of WORKS FOR is solid, indicating that *every* employee must work for some department. That is, EMPLOYEE's participation in WORKS FOR is universal. Similarly, the DEPARTMENT side of WORKS FOR is also solid, indicating that *every* department must have some employee working for it. In other words, DEPARTMENT fully participates in WORKS FOR.

The EMPLOYEE side of WORKS ON is dotted, indicating that *not all* employees (only *some*) work on projects. However, PROJECT's side of WORKS ON is solid, emphasizing that *every* project must have some employee working on it.

DEPARTMENT's participation in CONTROLS is partial, emphasizing that *not all* departments need to have projects under their control. However, projects must be always controlled by some

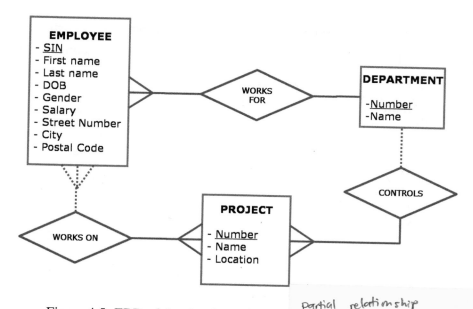

Figure 4.5: ERD of the simple company,

departments. That is, PROJECT fully participates in CONTR

[handwritten margin note]
partial relationship
~~that my dept~~
R — not all employees work on proj,
but every proj. must have some emp
working on it.

Not all dep. need to have
proj under their control.
However, projects must be
always controlled by some depts.

4.3   ERD Examples

On-line textbook selling

An on-line book selling service allows users to list their old
a textbook by its ISBN, title, or author. Users can also sea
including the school, department, course code, and semes
would be interested in, he/she can contact the seller by en
performed outside the service. However, users can rate the sellers.

An ERD for such a service is depicted in Figure 4.6. The entity-types are: BOOK, SELLER, and COURSE. BOOK and SELLER are related by the SELLS relationship-types. A seller can sell many books, but a particular book can be sold by only one seller. Notice that we have not used the ISBN as a primary key in BOOK since more than one copy of the same book have the same ISBN. SELLER's participation in SELLS is partial: not every registered seller must be selling some books. This is especially true for those who have signed up for the system but have not listed any books for sale yet. However, BOOK's participation in SELLS is full: every book listed in the service must be for sale (sold books are removed from the database).

TEXT relates BOOK and COURSE. This allows a buyer to search for a textbook by specifying course attributes. TEXT is many-to-many: the same book can be adopted by different courses, especially in different schools, and a course can have multiple textbooks. BOOK's participation in

TEXT is universal: the service does not list books unless they are adopted as textbooks somewhere. However, COURSE's participation in TEXT is partial: not all courses have corresponding books in the database.

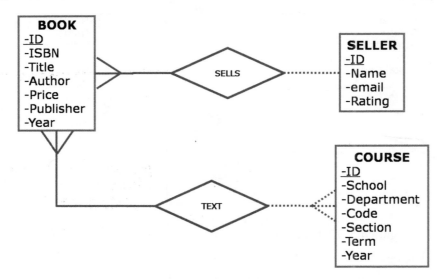

Figure 4.6: ERD for an on-line book selling service

Simple musical library

A musical library keeps track of music albums. An album can contain a collection of songs, and the library keeps information about all these songs, such as the duration and genre of a song. Singer information is also required. Figure 4.7 depicts an ERD for such a musical library (participation levels are omitted and are left to the reader as an exercise).

RECORDS is many-to-many: a singer can have many albums, and it is also possible for one album to contain songs from different singers. The CONTAINS relationship-type between ALBUM and SONG is one-to-many: an album typically has many songs, but a song should not be on more than one album (according to our model). Finally, the PERFORMS relationship-type is many-to-many since a singer can perform many songs, and a song can be performed by many singers (such as duets).

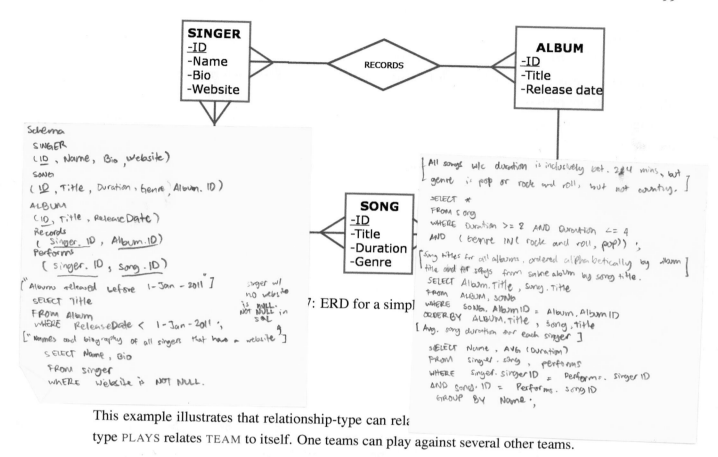

Schema
SINGER
(ID, Name, Bio, Website)
SONG
(ID, Title, Duration, Genre, Album.ID)
ALBUM
(ID, Title, Release Date)
Records
(Singer.ID, Album.ID)
Performs
(Singer.ID, Song.ID)

["Albums released before 1-Jan-2011"]
SELECT Title
FROM Album
WHERE ReleaseDate < 1-Jan-2011;
["Names and biography of all singers that have a website"]
SELECT Name, Bio
FROM singer
WHERE Website is NOT NULL.

singer w/
no website
is NULL.
NOT NULL in
SQL

[All songs w/c duration is inclusively bet. 2&4 mins, but
genre is pop or rock and roll, but not country.]
SELECT *
FROM song
WHERE Duration >= 2 AND Duration <= 4
AND (Genre IN(rock and roll, pop));
[Song titles for all albums, ordered alphabetically by album
title and for songs from same album by song title.]
SELECT Album.Title, Song.Title
FROM ALBUM, SONG
WHERE SONG.AlbumID = Album.AlbumID
ORDERBY ALBUM.Title, song.title
[Avg. song duration for each singer]
SELECT Name, AVG (Duration)
FROM singer.song, performs
WHERE singer.singerID = Performs.SingerID
AND Song.ID = Performs.SongID
GROUP BY Name;

7: ERD for a simpl

This example illustrates that relationship-type can rela
type PLAYS relates TEAM to itself. One teams can play against several other teams.

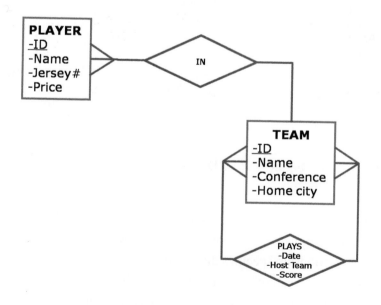

Figure 4.8: ERD for a basic sports tournament

Forestry database

Our last example is a data model for a forestry database, which keeps information about trees. Measurements are performed by employees on trees, counting the number of branches a tree has, its height, and its trunk width. The species of a tree and the forest in which the tree exists are also recorded.

Figure 4.9 shows an example of a forestry ERD. The participation levels here are also omitted and are left as an exercise.

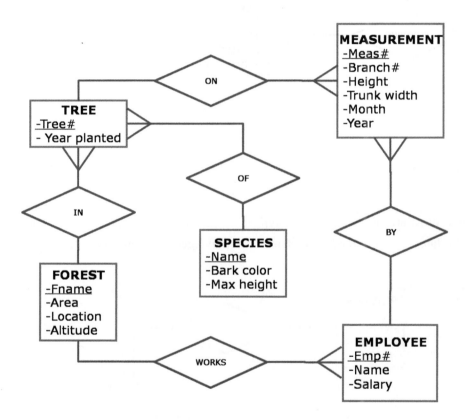

Figure 4.9: ERD for a forestry database

The IN relationship-type is one-to-many: a tree can be in exactly one forest, but a forest has many trees. OF is also one-to-many: a tree can be of only one species, but many trees can be of the same species. The ON relationship specifies that a measurement can be performed on one tree only, but a tree can have several measurements performed on it. Measurements are done BY employees. A measurement is performed by a single employee only, but an employee can perform several measurements. Finally, the WORKS relationship-type allows a forest to have several employees working in it, but an employee is assigned work in one forest only.

4.4 Mapping ERD to Schema

The ERD is one step toward designing a database. Once an ERD is designed, an algorithm can be followed to map the ERD to a database schema. First, we present the algorithm ignoring one-to-one relationship-types. The algorithm will be modified later to account for these relationship-types. The input to this algorithm is an ERD, and the output is a database schema.

Algorithm 4.1. — *Mapping simple ERD to schema* _____

Input: *an ERD*

Output: *a database schema*

1. *Each entity-type is translated to a table schema; the entity-types' attributes become columns in the corresponding table schema*

2. *Each many-to-many relationship-type becomes a table schema; the columns are the primary keys of the participating entity-types in the relationship-types; these are called* foreign keys

3. *For each one-to-many relationship-type, add the primary keys of the entity-type on the one-side as columns in the table-schema corresponding to the entity-type on the many-side; these are also called* foreign keys

We apply this algorithm to the ERD in Figure 4.5. There are three entity-types in this ERD. Applying step 1 results in the following schema:

EMPLOYEE

SIN	Fname	Lname	DOB	Gender	Salary	Snumber	Street	City	Pcode

DEPARTMENT

Dnumber	Dname

PROJECT

Pnumber	Pname	Location

Note that some attributes are given abbreviated names in the schema. For instance, Snumber abbreviates *street number* in EMPLOYEE.

There is only one many-to-many relationship-type. Applying step 2 of the algorithm yields an additional table schema, PROJ_EMP:

PROJ_EMP

SIN	Pnumber

The columns of PROJ_EMP are the primary keys of the participating entity-types: SIN of EM-PLOYEE and Pnumber of PROJECT.

Step 3 of the algorithm applies to one-to-many relationship-types. These do not cause the creation of new table schema, but they add columns to some of the existing schema. WORKS FOR is a one-to-many relationship-type with DEPARTMENT on the one-side and EMPLOYEE on the many-side. The algorithm dictates that we add the primary key of the entity-type on the one-side, DEPARTMENT, to the table corresponding to the entity-type on the many-side, EMPLOYEE. This results in the following updated schema for EMPLOYEE:

EMPLOYEE

SIN	Fname	Lname	DOB	Gender	Salary	Snumber	Street	City	Pcode	Dnumber

Similarly, CONTROLS augments the table schema PROJECT (the many-side) by adding to it the primary key of DEPARTMENT (the one-side):

PROJECT

Pnumber	Pname	Location	Dnumber

Notice that we have renamed number to Dnumber (for DEPARTMENT) and Pnumber (for PROJECT) to avoid any confusion when referring to the number of the project or the department. The same also applies to name (Dname and Pname).

One-to-one relationship-types

One-to-one relationship-types are rare in databases. Nevertheless, they can occur. For instance, a MANAGES relationship-type could be relating EMPLOYEE and DEPARTMENT. This relationship-type captures which employee *manages* which department. Since a department can have exactly one manager and an employee can manage only one department, this would be a one-to-one relationship-type. The updated ERD for the simple company database is depicted in Figure 4.10. Not all employees are managers, so EMPLOYEE's participation in MANAGES is partial. All departments have to have managers, so DEPARTMENT fully participates in MANAGES.

When mapping the ERD to schema, one-to-one relationship-types are treated like one-to-many relationship-types. They do not cause new table schema to be created. Instead, they augment the structure of some of the existing schema. With one-to-many relationship-types, the primary key on the one-side of the relationship-type is duplicated as a foreign key at the many-side of the

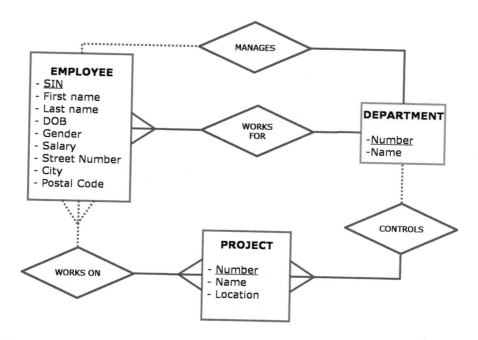

Figure 4.10: Updated simple company ERD, with the MANAGES relationship-type

relationship-type. One-to-one relationship-types are a little bit more difficult since both ends of a relationship-type are on a one-side. To guarantee a good design, we have to take participation levels into consideration. If the entity-types on both sides participate in the relationship-type at the same level (both are partial or both are full), then it does not matter which primary key is duplicated in the other end as a foreign key. It is your choice. However, if one entity-type's participation level is partial and the other's is full, we take the primary key of the partial-participation side and duplicate it as a foreign key in the table schema corresponding to the full-participation side. Later, we will justify this choice.

For instance, the MANAGES relationship-type of the ERD of Figure 4.10 causes the addition of the foreign key of the partial participation side (EMPLOYEE) in DEPARTMENT (on the full participation side) as follows:

DEPARTMENT

Dnumber	Dname	MGR_SIN

Attributes for relationship-types

We have given attributes to entity-types only, but relationship-types can also have attributes. Consider for instance the WORKS ON relationship-type. It simply tells us which employee is working on which project, but it does not tell us how many hours the employee is working on each project. To capture this extra information, the WORKS ON relationship-type must have an attribute, Hours. The number of hours an employee works on a project is not an attribute of EMPLOYEE nor of PROJECT. It is an attribute of the fact that an employee WORKS ON a project.

As another example, consider the MANAGES relationship-type of Figure 4.10. Here also, we may need to know the date that a manager assumed duties. If this is the case, then we need a Starting date of the MANAGES relationship-type.

The final version of the simple company ERD is given in Figure 4.11. Relationship-type attributes are listed inside the diamond shapes.

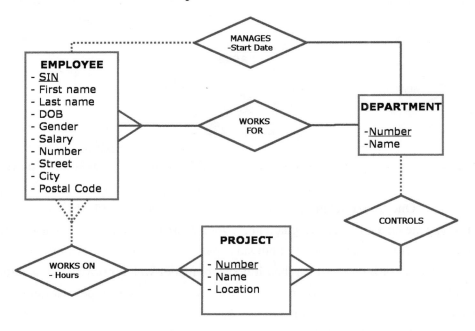

Figure 4.11: Final ERD for the simple company

Now, we are ready to refine the algorithm for mapping from ERD to a database schema so that it takes into consideration one-to-one relationship-types and relationship-type attributes.

Algorithm 4.2. — *Mapping ERD to schema* _____

Input: *an ERD*

Output: *a database schema*

1. *Each entity-type E is translated to a table schema T_E. T's columns are E's attributes.*

2. *Each many-to-many relationship-type R, relating entity-types E_1 and E_2, becomes a table schema T_R:*

   - *T_R's columns are R's attributes*

   - *the primary keys of E_1 and E_2 are added as columns in T_R*

3. *For each one-to-many relationship-type R, relating E_1 to E_2 with E_1 on the one-side:*

   - *add the primary key of E_1 as columns in T_{E_2}*
   - *any attributes that R has become columns in T_{E_2}*

4. *For each one-to-one relationship-type R, relating E_1 to E_2 with E_1 partially participating in R side or both E_1 and E_2 fully participate in R:*

   - *add the primary key of E_1 as columns in T_{E_2}*
   - *any attributes that R has become columns in T_{E_2}*

The resulting schema of the ERD in Figure 4.11 is in Figure 4.2.

4.5   Design Principles

What makes a database design good or bad? Why did we copy the primary key from the one-side of a relationship-type as a foreign key in the table corresponding to entity-type on the many-side? What if we do the opposite? These are some of the questions that are answered in this section. In general, there are three basic design principles in databases.

1. The meaning of a schema should be easily explained.

Do not combine attributes from different entity-types into a single table.

For instance, it would be tempting to combine both PROJECT and DEPARTMENT into one schema:

Dnumber	Dname	MGR_SIN	StartDate	Pnumber	Pname	Location

However, the resulting table would have an unclear meaning: is it a project table, a department table, or a controls table?

2. Reduce redundancy.

Unnecessary redundancy can lead to *modification anomalies*. Such anomalies arise when modification of data is required. Assume that we have designed the PROJECT schema as follows:

PROJECT

Pnumber	Pname	Location	Dnumber	Dname

The replication of Dname in PROJECT is unnecessary. A modification anomaly arises if the company decides to change the name of the *IT* department, say. Such a change will not be limited to DEPARTMENT, but it will need to be done in PROJECT and other tables where Dname is duplicated.

Note that in our original design of Figure 4.2, Dname occurs in only one place, the DEPARTMENT table, and any modification to it will be limited to the DEPARTMENT table. The remaining tables need not be changed.

As another example, let us consider the CONTROLS relationship-type. Assume instead of following our mapping algorithm, we copy the primary key of PROJECT in DEPARTMENT. This would result in the following schema:

PROJECT

Pnumber	Pname	Location

DEPARTMENT

Dnumber	Dname	MGR_SIN	StartDate	Pnumber

Our example database would contain:

DEPARTMENT

Dnumber	Dname	MGR_SIN	StartDate	Pnumber
1	IT	171717171	12-Feb-2008	1
1	IT	171717171	12-Feb-2008	2
2	Finance	123456789	1-Mar-2002	3
3	Marketing	666333999	1-Jan-2005	4

PROJECT

Pnumber	Pname	Location
1	Web Shopping	Calgary
2	Network Upgrade	Calgary
3	New Benefits	Toronto
4	Product XT345	Toronto

Since the *IT* department manages two projects, this results in two tuples corresponding to the *IT* department in DEPARTMENT. In general, this could result in much more redundancy, since it requires a department tuple for each project controlled by that department.

3. Reduce NULL values.

NULL values are blank values and are unavoidable, but the design should try to minimize them as much as possible. NULL values waste space. Also NULL values can result in confusion since a NULL value could mean several things: not applicable, unknown, or to be recorded. It is not always possible to determine the meaning of a NULL value.

Consider the MANAGES relationship-type. Assume that instead of following our mapping algorithm, we copy the primary key of DEPARTMENT in EMPLOYEE (the algorithm does the opposite). This would result in the following schema:

DEPARTMENT

Dnumber	Dname

EMPLOYEE

SIN	Fname	Lname	DOB	Gender	Salary	Snumber	Street	City	Pcode	Dnumber	MGR_Dnumber	StartDate

Since not all employees are managers (EMPLOYEE's participation in MANAGES is partial), this would result in unnecessary NULL values in EMPLOYEE:

EMPLOYEE

SIN	Fname	Lname	DOB	Gender	Salary	Snumber	Street	City	Pcode	Dnumber	MGR_Dnumber	StartDate
171717171	Debra	Beacon	15-Aug-1961	Female	70000	15	Baron Hill	Calgary	T2X Y0Y	1	1	12-Feb-2008
181817178	Sam	Field	17-Feb-1978	Male	40000	15	Kick Way	Calgary	Y2K K0K	1	NULL	NULL
123456789	Rajeet	Folk	30-Apr-1967	Male	78000	123	One Road	Toronto	H1H J9J	2	2	1-Mar-2002
987654321	Marie	Band	12-Jan-1985	Female	53500	2828	Exit Close	Toronto	K8O O8K	2	NULL	NULL
666333999	Saleh	Dice	25-Mar-1970	Male	90400	66	Straight Way	Toronto	T4E T6B	3	3	1-Jan-2005

Algorithm 4.2 adheres to these three design principles. However, for the algorithm to generate good design, it must start from a good ERD. Otherwise, the old saying "*garbage in, garbage out*" stands.

By the Way — Microsoft Access _____

Microsoft Access is a *database management* application program. It facilitates the creation and use of a database. In this section, we will focus on basic operations in Microsoft Access 2007, such as how to create and populate tables. The following section will discuss queries in detail.

To create a new database file, start Microsoft Access, choose *blank database*, and click create.

Creating tables

To create a table in Microsoft Access, click the *create* ribbon, then choose *Table*. A new table is created:

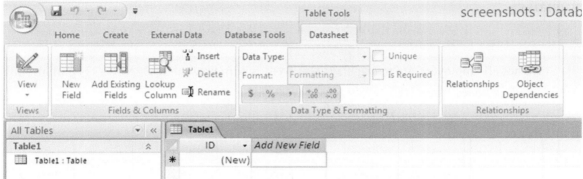

Right click the newly created table tab and choose save. Access prompts you for a name. Give the table a meaningful name:

Tables can viewed in different ways. Pull down the *view* menu  and choose the *Design* view:

In the design view, fill in the table column names in *Field Name* and their data types in *Data Type*:

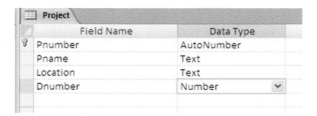

There are several data types in Access: Text, Number, Date/Time, Yes/No, etc.

Note that Pnumber has a key symbol beside it, indicating that it is a primary key. Access requires every table to have a primary key. To change the primary key, right click the desired *Field Name*, and choose *Primary Key*.

To populate a table with data, switch to the *Datasheet* view, and fill in the table:

Pnumber	Pname	Location	Dnumber	Add New Field
1	Web Shopping	Calgary	1	
2	Network Upgra	Calgary	1	
3	New Benefits	Toronto	2	
4	Product XT345			
(New)				

Save the table. Note that the *AutoNumber* data type is not fillable by the user; instead, it is automatically filled in by Access.

Creating relationships

To create a relationship between tables, choose the *Database Tools* ribbon, and click relationships:

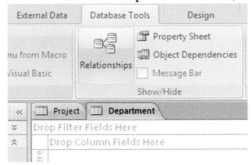

From the *Show Table* window, choose the tables involved in the relationship and click *add*:

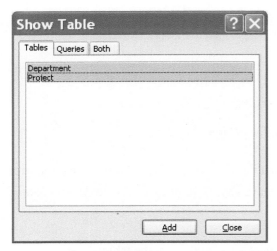

Close the table window. We will establish the CONTROLS relationship. Drag Dnumber from DE-PARTMENT and drop it on Dnumber in PROJECT. The *Edit relationship* window appears:

Click *create*. The relationship is established:

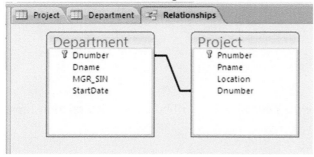

Creating queries

To create a query, choose *Query Design* from the *Create* ribbon:

Choose the table (or tables) on which the query will be performed from the *Show Table* window:

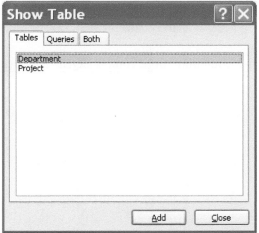

Click *Add*.

In this example, we will retrieve Pnumber, Pname, and Location of the projects that are located in Calgary. In the *Query Formulation* window, select the fields required for the query (Pnumber, Pname, and Location):

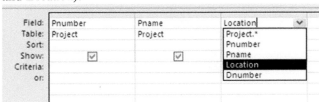

Enter *Calgary* in the *Criteria* row under Location:

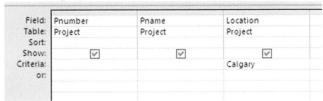

Press the *Run* button to view the query result:

Save your query with a meaningful name.

The way by which this query was created is called *Query By Example* (QBE). Queries can also be formulated by writing a small SQL program. To see the program corresponding to the query that was just created, choose *SQL View* from the *View* menu:

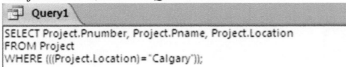

The next section focuses on the SQL language as well as formulating more complex QBE queries.

4.6 Queries

Simple queries can be formulated using QBE; however, more complex queries may require writing the query directly in SQL. SQL stands for *Structured Query Language*. It is an English-like computer language that is specific for databases. The language has two parts: the Data Definition Language (DDL) used to define the database such as the table structure and the Data Manipulation Language (DML) used to insert, delete, modify, and query data (contents of the tables). A query is a question submitted to the database, and the answer is a relation (a collection of tuples). In this section, we will only address the queries part of DML. Other DML statements and some DDL statements are covered later in the chapter.

4.6.1 Basic queries

A basic SQL query has the clauses SELECT, FROM, and WHERE. The FROM clause specifies which tables the query is being performed on, and the SELECT clause specifies the columns that need to be returned. The WHERE clause is optional and specifies a Boolean condition. Only those tuples that satisfy the Boolean condition will be returned. The general syntax of a basic SELECT statement is:

```
SELECT    list of columns
FROM      list of tables
WHERE     Boolean condition
```

The *list of columns* must be from tables in the *list of tables*. The Boolean condition should be also formulated on columns of the tables in the *list of tables*.

SQL is better introduced by examples. We will use the database of Figure 4.1 for all of our query examples.

Example 4.1

When the WHERE condition is omitted from a SELECT statement, the operation is called *projection*. The following SQL statement projects DEPARTMENT on two columns only:

```
SELECT    Dnumber, Dname
FROM      DEPARTMENT;
```

That is, the answer to the query is:

Dnumber	Dname
1	IT
2	Finance
3	Marketing

SQL statements are always terminated by a semicolon.

In general, SQL queries require a WHERE clause which filters the returned tuples in the query result. When a WHERE clause is used, the operation is called *selection*.

Example 4.2

The following SQL statement selects from PROJECT only those projects that are located in *Calgary*:

```
SELECT    Pnumber, Pname, Location, Dnumber
FROM      PROJECT
WHERE     Location = 'Calgary';
```

The result of this query is:

Pnumber	Pname	Location	Dnumber
1	Web Shopping	Calgary	1
2	New Benefits	Calgary	1

There is a cleaner way to write this same query. Instead of listing all the columns of PROJECT, we can simply use the wild card ⋆:

```
SELECT    *
FROM      PROJECT
WHERE     Location = 'Calgary';
```

The ⋆ is interpreted as all the columns of all the tables in the FROM clause.

Most of the time, queries combine selection and projection together.

Example 4.3

The query:

```
SELECT   Pnumber, Pname
FROM     PROJECT
WHERE    Location = 'Calgary';
```

returns:

Pnumber	Pname
1	Web Shopping
2	New benefits

In Microsoft Access QBE, restricting the selected columns is performed in the *Query Formulation* window. For instance, this SQL query can be formulated as an Access QBE as follows:

Field:	Pnumber	Pname	Location
Table:	Project	Project	Project
Sort:			
Show:	☑	☑	☐
Criteria:			"Calgary"
or:			

Note that Location's *Show* check-box is de-selected, and it will not show in the query result. Yet, it is needed to formulate the *Criteria* (Location = 'Calgary').

4.6.2 Set operations

The result of a query is a relation, which is a set. SQL allows us to combine the sets resulting from two different queries into one set using operations: union, intersection, and difference. The general structure of such queries is:

Query1
Set operation
Query2

The *set operation* is one of: UNION, INTERSECT, or MINUS.

Example 4.4

The following query returns the names of all employees whose salary is more than $80,000 in addition to those who work for department 1:

```
SELECT    Fname, Lname
FROM      EMPLOYEE
WHERE     Salary > 80000
UNION
SELECT    Fname, Lname
FROM      EMPLOYEE
WHERE     Dnumber = 1;
```

Its result is shown best in this Venn diagram:

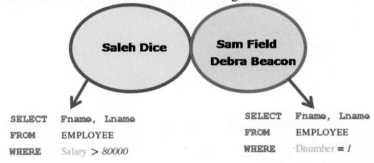

The result of the following query is the names of all female employees who live in Calgary:

```
SELECT        Fname, Lname
FROM          EMPLOYEE
WHERE         Gender = 'Female'
INTERSECT
SELECT        Fname, Lname
FROM          EMPLOYEE
WHERE         City = 'Calgary';
```

This result is also shown best by a Venn diagram:

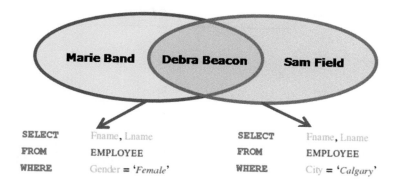

SELECT	Fname, Lname		SELECT	Fname, Lname
FROM	EMPLOYEE		FROM	EMPLOYEE
WHERE	Gender = 'Female'		WHERE	City = 'Calgary'

The following query retrieves the SIN of all non-manager males:

SELECT	SIN
FROM	EMPLOYEE
WHERE	Gender = 'Male'
MINUS	
SELECT	MGR_SIN
FROM	DEPARTMENT;

Its result is given by the Venn diagram:

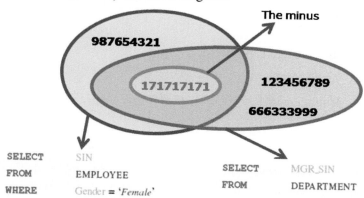

SELECT	SIN		SELECT	MGR_SIN
FROM	EMPLOYEE		FROM	DEPARTMENT
WHERE	Gender = 'Female'			

Microsoft Access supports the UNION set operation only. Union queries cannot be formulated as QBE queries. They must be formulated in the *SQL View*.

Recall that if A is a set, then $a \in A$ is true when a is an element in A. SQL has an IN construct, which is similar to set membership. The next example illustrates the use of IN.

Example 4.5

```
SELECT    Fname, Lname
FROM      EMPLOYEE
WHERE     Gender = 'Male'
AND       SIN IN
              (SELECT    MGR_SIN
               FROM      DEPARTMENT);
```

First the result of the "main" query is determined, without considering IN:

```
SELECT    Fname, Lname
FROM      EMPLOYEE
WHERE     Gender = 'Male'
```

This query returns the names of all *Male* employees. In particular, these employees' SINs are in the set *Males* = { *181817178*, *123456789*, *666333999* }. Then, the result of the "sub-query" is determined:

```
SELECT    MGR_SIN
FROM      DEPARTMENT
```

This gives the SINs for managers, or the set:

$$Managers = \{ \; 171717171, \, 123456789, \, 666333999 \; \}.$$

For each element in *Males*, the IN construct checks if it is also *in Managers*. If this is the case, the name of this employee is returned. If not, it will be skipped. For instance *181817178* $\notin$ *Managers*, and the employee with this SIN, *Sam Field*, will not be returned. However, The names of the employees with the SINs *123456789* and *666333999* will be returned. Hence, this query returns the names of male managers.

The IN construct works like the INTERSECT. Similar to UNION, Microsoft Access supports IN; however, you can use it with directly with QBE queries.

The MINUS operation can be emulated using the negation of IN. For instance the MINUS query of Example 4.5 can be formulated as follows:

```
SELECT    SIN
FROM      EMPLOYEE
WHERE     Gender = 'Male'
AND       SIN NOT IN
                (SELECT    MGR_SIN
                 FROM      DEPARTMENT);
```

This will only return the SINs of the employees whose SIN is not in the set *Managers*.

Complex Boolean conditions

The WHERE clause can include complex Boolean conditions using the logic operations: AND, OR, and NOT. The comparison operators used in SQL are:

Equals	=
Greater than	>
Less than	<
Different (not equal to)	!= or <>
Less than or equal to	<=
Greater than or equal to	>=

Example 4.6

The following query retrieves the last names and dates of birth of female employees whose salary is more than 40K:

```
SELECT    Lname, DOB
FROM      EMPLOYEE
WHERE     Gender = 'Female'
          AND Salary > 40000;
```

In Access QBE, the query can be formulated as:

Field:	Lname	DOB	Gender	Salary
Table:	EMPLOYEE	EMPLOYEE	EMPLOYEE	EMPLOYEE
Sort:				
Show:	☑	☑	☐	☐
Criteria:			'Female'	>40000
or:				

Criteria across columns (such as Salary > 40000 and Gender = 'Female') are combined with the *and* operator.

The following query retrieves the SIN, last name, and first name of employees whose salary is between (inclusive) 30K and 50K:

```
SELECT    SIN, Lname, Fname
FROM      EMPLOYEE
WHERE     Salary >= 30000
          AND Salary <= 50000;
```

The QBE version is:

Field:	Sin	Lname	Fname	Salary
Table:	EMPLOYEE	EMPLOYEE	EMPLOYEE	EMPLOYEE
Sort:				
Show:	☑	☑	☑	☐
Criteria:				>=30000 And <=5000
or:				

Note that the *and* must be explicitly used in *Criteria* since the anded conditions apply to the same column.

The following query retrieves the SIN, last name, and first name of all male employees who earn more than 30K and all female employees who earn above 40K:

```
SELECT    SIN, Lname, Fname
FROM      EMPLOYEE
WHERE     ( Gender = 'Male' AND Salary > 30000 )
          OR ( Gender = 'Female' AND Salary > 40000 ) ;
```

The QBE version is as follows:

Field:	SIN	Lname	Fname	Gender	Salary
Table:	EMPLOYEE	EMPLOYEE	EMPLOYEE	EMPLOYEE	EMPLOYEE
Sort:					
Show:	☑	☑	☑	☐	☐
Criteria:				"Male"	>30000
or:				"Female"	>40000

Alternatively, the same query can be expressed using set union as follows:

```
SELECT    SIN, Lname, Fname
FROM      EMPLOYEE
WHERE     Gender = 'Male'
          AND Salary > 30000
UNION
SELECT    SIN, Lname, Fname
FROM      EMPLOYEE
WHERE     Gender = 'Female'
          AND Salary > 40000;
```

Contradiction and tautology conditions

When formulating an SQL condition, a common mistake for beginners is to use contradiction and tautology conditions. For instance, the query:

```
SELECT    *
FROM      EMPLOYEE
WHERE     Gender = 'Male'
          OR Gender = Female;
```

is equivalent to:

```
SELECT    *
FROM      EMPLOYEE;
```

since the condition (Gender = 'Male') OR (Gender = Female) is a tautology. Every employee has one of these Genders.

On the other hand, the following query:

```
SELECT    *
FROM      EMPLOYEE
WHERE     Gender = 'Male'
          AND Gender = Female;
```

will always have an empty result because the condition (Gender = 'Male') AND (Gender = Female) is a contradiction. According to our database, no employee can have both Gender values simultaneously.

While in these examples the contradiction or tautology is obvious, they may not be so in more complex queries. For instance, the following query has a tautology condition:

```
SELECT    *
FROM      EMPLOYEE
WHERE     NOT (Gender = 'Male'
              AND ( Salary > 40000 AND Gender ! = Male ));
```

Let g = Gender = 'Male and s = Salary > 40000. The WHERE condition can be written as follows:

$\neg(g \wedge (s \wedge \neg g))$. A truth table can quickly reveal that this proposition is a tautology. Alternatively, it is equivalent to:

$\neg g \vee \neg(s \wedge \neg g)$, using DeMorgan's rule. This is also equivalent to:

$\neg g \vee (\neg s \vee \neg\neg g)$, using DeMorgan's again. After we eliminate double negation, it becomes:

$\neg g \vee (\neg s \vee g)$. Applying the associative rules:

$(\neg g \lor \neg g) \lor s$, which is equivalent to:

$T \lor s$, which also always true by domination.

4.6.3   Join queries

So far, in all the queries that were considered, the FROM clause consists of one table only. Join queries take advantage of how data in different tables is related. For instance, PROJECT has the foreign key Dnumber which relates to DEPARTMENT. If we need to know which department controls the *Web Shopping* project, from table PROJECT it can be determined that it is department number *1*. Another query is required from table DEPARTMENT to figure out the rest of the department information, such as the department name. SQL allows us to formulate such queries in one shot using *natural joins*.

Example 4.7

Consider the following query:

```
SELECT   *
FROM     PROJECT, DEPARTMENT;
```

This query gives us the *product* of the set PROJECT and the set DEPARTMENT, or PROJECT × DEPARTMENT. In other words, this query pairs each project with every department, whether they are related or not. The result is:

Pnumber	Pname	Location	Dnumber	Dnumber	Dname	MGR_SIN	StartDate
1	Web Shopping	Calgary	1	1	IT	171717171	12-Feb-2008
1	Web Shopping	Calgary	1	2	Finance	123456789	1-Mar-2002
1	Web Shopping	Calgary	1	3	Marketing	666333999	1-Jan-2005
2	Network Upgrade	Calgary	1	1	IT	171717171	12-Feb-2008
2	Network Upgrade	Calgary	1	2	Finance	123456789	1-Mar-2002
2	Network Upgrade	Calgary	1	3	Marketing	666333999	1-Jan-2005
3	New Benefits	Toronto	2	1	IT	171717171	12-Feb-2008
3	New Benefits	Toronto	2	2	Finance	123456789	1-Mar-2002
3	New Benefits	Toronto	2	3	Marketing	666333999	1-Jan-2005
4	Product XT345	Toronto	3	1	IT	171717171	12-Feb-2008
4	Product XT345	Toronto	3	2	Finance	123456789	1-Mar-2002
4	Product XT345	Toronto	3	3	Marketing	666333999	1-Jan-2005

A query like this is not useful by itself. We need to further filter the results, leaving only the meaningful project-department pairs. For instance, it makes sense to keep only the *IT* department beside the *Web Shopping* project because the latter is controlled by the *IT* department. That is, we want the Dnumber of PROJECT to be the same as the Dnumber from DEPARTMENT. The matching values were highlighted in the above table.

To eliminate the rows where DEPARTMENT.Dnumber and PROJECT.Dnumber do not match, we add a WHERE clause to filter these rows out:

```
SELECT   *
FROM     PROJECT, DEPARTMENT
WHERE    PROJECT.Dnumber = DEPARTMENT.Dnumber;
```

This is called a *natural join*, and the result of the query is:

Pnumber	Pname	Location	Dnumber	Dnumber	Dname	MGR_SIN	StartDate
1	Web Shopping	Calgary	1	1	IT	171717171	12-Feb-2008
2	Network Upgrade	Calgary	1	1	IT	171717171	12-Feb-2008
3	New Benefits	Toronto	2	2	Finance	123456789	1-Mar-2002
4	Product XT345	Toronto	3	3	Marketing	666333999	1-Jan-2005

Example 4.8

The following query retrieves the addresses of all employees who work for the IT department:

```
SELECT   Snumber, Street, City, Pcode
FROM     EMPLOYEE, DEPARTMENT
WHERE    EMPLOYEE.Dnumber = DEPARTMENT.Dnumber
         AND Dname = 'IT';
```

Join conditions in QBE queries are easy to formulate in Microsoft Access if a relationship between the tables has already been established in the database. For instance, the WORKS FOR and MANAGES relationships are already established:

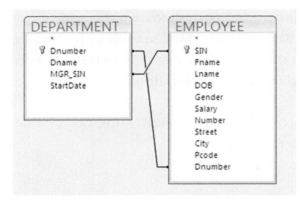

This query will join these tables on both relationships by default. Since MANAGES is irrelevant to this query, click it and delete it:

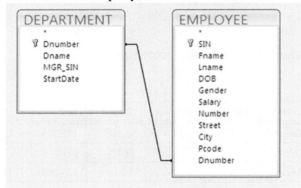

The query can then be formulated as follows:

Field:	Number	Street	City	Pcode	Dname
Table:	EMPLOYEE	EMPLOYEE	EMPLOYEE	EMPLOYEE	DEPARTMENT
Sort:					
Show:	☑	☑	☑	☑	☑
Criteria:					
or:					'IT'

Note that the Microsoft Access generated SQL code (from the QBE join query) differs from the standard we are referring to:

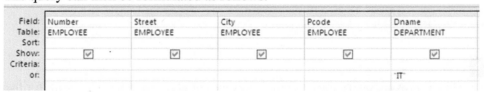

```
SELECT EMPLOYEE.Number, EMPLOYEE.Street, EMPLOYEE.City, EMPLOYEE.Pcode, DEPARTMENT.Dname
FROM DEPARTMENT INNER JOIN EMPLOYEE ON DEPARTMENT.Dnumber = EMPLOYEE.Dnumber
WHERE (((DEPARTMENT.Dname)='IT'));
```

Yet the standard we are using can be entered directly in the *SQL View*, and Microsoft Access does accept it.

Determining the result of a join query

Determining the result of a query with a join condition can be tedious. Consider the following query:

SELECT	SIN, Snumber, Street, City, Pcode, Dname
FROM	EMPLOYEE, DEPARTMENT
WHERE	EMPLOYEE.Dnumber = DEPARTMENT.Dnumber
	AND Dname = 'Marketing'
	AND Salary > 70000;

One straightforward way is to start determining the result by considering the Cartesian product of EMPLOYEE and DEPARTMENT. If EMPLOYEE has n tuples and DEPARTMENT has m tuples, we would be starting with a result set of $n \times m$ tuples. In our case, this is $6 \times 3 = 18$ tuples, but in general this could be prohibitively large. The last two lines of the SQL query can restrict the result set since we need not consider all departments and all employees. There is exactly one department with Dname = 'Marketing' and we only have two employees whose salary > 70K. So, we need only work with $2 \times 1 = 2$ tuples to construct the result of this query. So, we build the result starting by applying the filtering imposed by the last two lines.

The table DEPARTMENT when filtered by Dname = 'Marketing', leaves us with the following subset of DEPARTMENT:

Dnumber	Dname	MGR_SIN	StartDate
3	Marketing	666333999	1-Jan-2005

Similarly, applying the condition Salary > 70000 gives us the following subset of EMPLOYEE:

SIN	Fname	Lname	DOB	Gender	Salary	Snumber	Street	City	Pcode	Dnumber
123456789	Rajeet	Folk	30-Apr-1967	Male	78000	123	One Road	Toronto	H1H J9J	2
666333999	Saleh	Dice	25-Mar-1970	Male	90400	66	Straight Way	Toronto	T4E T6B	3

The Cartesian product is now simpler to work with:

SIN	Snumber	Street	City	Pcode	Dnumber	Dnumber	Dname
123456789	123	One Road	Toronto	H1H J9J	2	3	Marketing
666333999	66	Straight Way	Toronto	T4E T6B	3	3	Marketing

Applying the join condition, we quickly infer that the result of this query is:

SIN	Snumber	Street	City	Pcode	Dname
666333999	66	Straight Way	Toronto	T4E T6B	Marketing

Ordering the query result

The rows returned as a result for a query are ordered in the way they are stored in the database. We can instruct the SQL query to order the result using an ORDER BY clause. This clause must follow the WHERE clause, if it exists, or the FROM clause if the WHERE clause does not exist.

Example 4.9

The following query orders the result by last name:

```
SELECT      *
FROM        EMPLOYEE
WHERE       City != 'Calgary'
ORDER BY    Lname ASC;
```

Using Access QBE, the query is:

Field:	EMPLOYEE.*	Lname	City
Table:	EMPLOYEE	EMPLOYEE	EMPLOYEE
Sort:		Ascending	
Show:	☑	☐	☐
Criteria:			<>"Calgary"
or:			

Simply indicate in the *Sort* row whether you want the result sorted according to a certain column whether you want it listed in *ascending* or *descending* order.

The following query orders the result by last name in descending order:

```
SELECT      *
FROM        EMPLOYEE
WHERE       City != 'Calgary'
ORDER BY    Lname DESC;
```

The following query orders the result by last name and then by first name (if two employees have the same last name, the tie is broken by their first names):

```
SELECT      *
FROM        EMPLOYEE
WHERE       City != 'Calgary'
ORDER BY    Lname, Fname ASC;
```

4.6.4 Aggregate functions

Aggregate or group functions perform calculations on a group of tuples. Some of the aggregate functions in SQL are:

- SUM: sum of values in a column

- AVG: average of values in a column

- COUNT: number of not-null values in a column

- MIN: minimum value in a column

- MAX: maximum value in a column

Note the similarities between these functions and the functions in Microsoft Excel.

Example 4.10

The following query determines the sum of all salaries:

```
SELECT   SUM (Salary)
FROM     EMPLOYEE;
```

The group functions in Access QBE are indicated in the *Total* row:

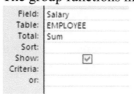

The following query determines the number of records in EMPLOYEE:

```
SELECT   COUNT (SIN)
FROM     EMPLOYEE;
```

The following query determines the average salary in the *IT* department:

```
SELECT    AVG (Salary)
FROM      EMPLOYEE, DEPARTMENT
WHERE     EMPLOYEE.Dnumber = DEPARTMENT.Dnumber
          AND Dname = 'IT';
```

The following query determines the minimum salary for female employees who work for the *Finance* department:

```
SELECT    MIN (Salary)
FROM      EMPLOYEE, DEPARTMENT
WHERE     EMPLOYEE.Dnumber = DEPARTMENT.Dnumber
          AND Dname = 'Finance'
          AND Gender = 'Female';
```

The following query determines the maximum salary among employees who work on projects located in Toronto:

```
SELECT    MAX (Salary)
FROM      EMPLOYEE, PROJ_EMP, PROJECT
WHERE     EMPLOYEE.SIN = PROJ_EMP.SIN
          AND PROJECT.Pnumber = PROJ_EMP.Pnumber
          AND Location = 'Toronto';
```

Grouping calculations

A GROUP BY clause in SQL allows the application of aggregate functions for separate groups of tuples, such as counting the number of employees in each department. That is, it groups tuples into subsets and then applies the aggregate function to each subset separately. The GROUP BY clause follows the WHERE clause (or the FROM clause if there is no WHERE clause).

Example 4.11

The following query determines the sum of all salaries for each department:

```
SELECT    Dnumber, SUM (Salary)
FROM      EMPLOYEE
GROUP BY  Dnumber;
```

The result is:

Dnumber	SUM (Salary)
1	*11000*
2	*131500*
3	*90400*

In QBE, GROUP BY is indicated also in the *Total* row. The above query can be formulated in Access QBE as follows:

Field:	Dnumber	Salary
Table:	EMPLOYEE	EMPLOYEE
Total:	Group By	Sum
Sort:		
Show:	☑	☑
Criteria:		
or:		

The following query calculates the average salary per gender:

SELECT   Gender, AVG (Salary)
FROM   EMPLOYEE
GROUP BY   Gender;

We can further filter the result of a group function by requiring that the aggregate value satisfy a certain Boolean condition. This can be done by the HAVING clause.

Example 4.12

The following query determines the number of projects that each employee works on:

SELECT   SIN, COUNT (Pnumber)
FROM   PROJ_EMP
GROUP BY   SIN;

The following query further filters the result to include only those employees who work on more than one project:

SELECT   SIN, COUNT (Pnumber)
FROM   PROJ_EMP
GROUP BY   SIN
HAVING   COUNT (Pnumber) > *1*;

The QBE version of this query is:

Field:	Sin	Proj_Count: Count(*)	
Table:	PROJ_EMP		
Total:	Group By	Expression	
Sort:			
Show:	☑	☑	
Criteria:		>1	
or:			

4.6.5 Logic quantifiers in SQL

Query conditions can become quite complex, requiring logic quantifiers. For instance, how would one formulate the query that retrieves all the employees who work on *every* project that is located in Calgary?

Recall that in predicate logic there are two types of quantifiers: universal and existential. Also, recall that one form of quantification can be expressed using the other. In particular, $\forall x P(x)$ is logically equivalent to $\neg \exists x \neg P(x)$.

SQL provides a construct equivalent to the existential quantifier. It does not provide a construct that is equivalent to universal quantification. Nevertheless, the latter can always be expressed using existential quantification. The existential quantifier in SQL is provided through the EXISTS function. This function can be used in the WHERE clause. The argument to EXISTS(Q) is a select statement Q. The return value of EXISTS(Q) is true if Q has a non-empty result; it is false otherwise.

Example 4.13

The following query retrieves the projects that are controlled by the Marketing department:

```
SELECT   *
FROM     PROJECT
WHERE    EXISTS (
                SELECT   *
                FROM     DEPARTMENT
                WHERE    PROJECT.Dnumber = DEPARTMENT.Dnumber
                         AND Dname = 'Marketing'
         );
```

If the inner query (on DEPARTMENT) returns any values, the EXIST function returns true. Note how the condition in the inner query depends on the table PROJECT in the outer query.

EXIST is not supported by Microsoft Access. However, EXIST queries can be mimicked using IN, which is supported in Microsoft Access. For instance, the same query can be written as:

```
SELECT   *
FROM     PROJECT
WHERE    Dnumber IN (
              SELECT   Dnumber
              FROM     DEPARTMENT
              WHERE    Dname = 'Marketing'
              ) ;
```

In fact, the same query can be expressed in an easier way using a natural join:

```
SELECT   *
FROM     PROJECT, DEPARTMENT
WHERE    PROJECT.Dnumber = DEPARTMENT.Dnumber
         AND Dname = 'Marketing' ;
```

One might be wondering why one would want to use the EXISTS function if an easier alternative (natural joins) can be used. The importance of EXISTS is that it allows universal quantification to be formulated in the query condition, and natural joins cannot be used for such conditions. The next question develops an SQL statement for the following query:

Retrieve the departments who have *only* female employees.

In other words, we need to retrieve only the departments whose employees are *all* female. If a department has at least one male employee, they have to be filtered out from the query result.

Example 4.14

One tempting (but **wrong**) attempt is to write this query as such:

```
SELECT   Dnumber, Dname
FROM     DEPARTMENT, EMPLOYEE
WHERE    DEPARTMENT.Dnumber = EMPLOYEE.Dnumber
         AND Gender = 'Female' ;
```

This query returns the departments who have at *least one* female employee. In other words, The quantification on female employees is existential. However, the original requirement universally quantifies female employees. The condition "departments who have *only* female employees" can be expressed in predicate logic and set notation as follows:

All-Female-Departments =
$\{d|$ DEPARTMENT$(d) \land \forall e(($EMPLOYEE$(e) \land$ WORKS_FOR$(e,d)) \to e.$Gender $=$ '*Female*' $)\}$

The predicate DEPARTMENT(d) means d is a department; EMPLOYEE(e) means e is an employee; and WORKS_FOR(e,d) means e works for d. Hence, All-Female-Departments is the set of all d such that d is a department, and any employee e who works for department d must be a female. Recall that the WORKS FOR relationship-type is determined by the condition:
$e.$Dnumber $= d.$Dnumber
So:

All-Female-Departments =
$\{d|$ DEPARTMENT$(d) \land \forall e (($EMPLOYEE$(e) \land e.$Dnumber $= d.$Dnumber$) \to e.$Gender $=$ '*Female*' $)\}$

Since SQL does not have direct support for implication, we need to re-write this query and replace $a \to b$ with its logically equivalent disjunctive form, $\neg a \lor b$:

All-Female-Departments =
$\{d|$ DEPARTMENT$(d) \land \forall e(\neg($EMPLOYEE$(e) \land e.$Dnumber $= d.$Dnumber$) \lor e.$Gender $=$ '*Female*'$)\}$

Since SQL does not have a universal quantifier function, we need to re-write this query so that it uses only existential quantifiers. That is, $\forall x P(x)$ is replaced by $\neg \exists x \neg P(x)$:

All-Female-Departments =
$\{d|$ DEPARTMENT$(d) \land \neg \exists e \neg(\neg($EMPLOYEE$(e) \land e.$Dnumber $= d.$Dnumber$) \lor e.$Gender $=$ '*Female*'$)\}$

Simplifying, using DeMorgan's rules:

All-Female-Departments =

$\{d|\ \text{DEPARTMENT}(d) \land \lnot\exists e(\lnot\lnot(\text{EMPLOYEE}(e) \land e.\text{Dnumber} = d.\text{Dnumber}) \land \lnot(e.\text{Gender} = \text{`Female'})\}$

Eliminating double negation and re-writing:

All-Female-Departments $=$

$\{d|\ \text{DEPARTMENT}(d) \land \lnot\exists e((\text{EMPLOYEE}(e) \land e.\text{Dnumber} = d.\text{Dnumber}) \land (e.\text{Gender} \neq \text{`Female'})\}$

That is, this is the set of all departments d that do not have a single employee who works for d and that employee is not a female. Now we can easily write this query in SQL:

```
SELECT   *
FROM     DEPARTMENT
WHERE    NOT EXISTS (
                SELECT   *
                FROM     EMPLOYEE
                WHERE    EMPLOYEE.Dnumber = DEPARTMENT.Dnumber
                         AND Gender != 'Female'
                );
```

Re-writing the query with IN instead of EXISTS yields:

```
SELECT   *
FROM     DEPARTMENT
WHERE    Dnumber NOT IN (
                SELECT   Dnumber
                FROM     EMPLOYEE
                WHERE    Gender != 'Female'
                );
```

Since our database has no only-female departments, this returns an empty result when run on our database.

4.7 Other SQL Statements

4.7.1 Creating and deleting tables

The most important DDL statement in SQL is the statement that creates a table. Unlike small applications like MS Access, large Database Management Systems (DBMS) require the use of SQL to create and populate tables. These include Oracle DBMS and Microsoft SQL Server.

In SQL, each table is created by a separate `CREATE` statement, which specifies the table name and the names and types of columns. The basic column types are `NUMBER`, `CHAR`, and `DATE`. The type `NUMBER` can specify integers or floating point numbers. Adding one argument `NUMBER(n)` specifies the type as an integer of up to n digits. Adding two arguments `NUMBER(n,m)` specifies a floating point number of up to n digits with m fractional digits (to the right of the decimal point). The `CHAR` type can also have an argument that specifies the length of the string, which is the number of characters in the string.

The general syntax of a `CREATE` is as follows:

```
CREATE TABLE TABLE-NAME
( column1-name   column1-type,
  column2-name   column2-type,
  ...
  columnN-name   columnN-type ) ;
```

Figure 4.12 shows the statements that create the database schema of Figure 4.2.

The second DDL statement that we discuss here is the `DROP` statement which entirely deletes a table from the database. The general syntax of a `DROP` is as follows:

```
DROP TABLE TABLE-NAME;
```

There are other DDL statements and features, but they are not discussed in this book.

4.7.2 Adding and deleting tuples

In addition to the `SELECT` DML statement, we will only discuss two other basic DML statements here: `INSERT` to insert tuples to a table and `DELETE` to delete tuples from a table.

The `INSERT` statement has the syntax:

```
INSERT INTO TABLE-NAME VALUES  ( list of values ) ;
```

```
CREATE TABLE EMPLOYEE
(
 SIN        NUMBER(9),
 Fname      CHAR(15),
 Lname      CHAR(15),
 DOB        DATE,
 Gender     CHAR(6),
 Salary     NUMBER,
 Snumber    NUMBER(10),
 Street     CHAR(30),
 City       CHAR(15),
 Pcode      CHAR(7),
 Dnumber    NUMBER
);

CREATE TABLE DEPARTMENT
(
 Dnumber    NUMBER),
 Dname      CHAR(20),
 MGR_SIN    CHAR(9),
 StartDate  DATE
);

CREATE TABLE PROJECT
(
 Pnumber    NUMBER,
 Pname      CHAR(30),
 Location   CHAR(15),
 Dnumber    NUMBER
);

CREATE TABLE PROJ_EMP
(
 SIN        CHAR(9),
 Pnumber    NUMBER,
 Hours      NUMBER
);
```

Figure 4.12: Creating the database schema of Figure 4.2

The *list of values* must have a value for each column in TABLE-NAME, and these must be in the same order used in the CREATE statement when the table was created. CHAR and DATE values must be enclosed by single quotes, but quotes are not required for NUMBER.

Each tuple must be inserted by a separate INSERT statement. For instance, the following statement adds the *IT* department to DEPARTMENT:

INSERT INTO DEPARTMENT VALUES (*1*, '*IT*', *171717171*, '*12-Feb-2008*') ;

Figure 4.13 shows how to populate the database schema of Figure 4.2 to become the database of Figure 4.1.

The DELETE statement deletes tuples from a table, but it does not delete the table itself. To entirely delete the table (the contents and the table itself), a DROP statement must be used. To delete all the tuples in a table, the DELETE statement has the syntax:

DELETE FROM TABLE-NAME;

To delete a subset of the tuples, the DELETE statement requires an additional WHERE clause:

DELETE FROM TABLE-NAME
WHERE *Boolean-condition*;

Only the tuples that satisfy the *Boolean-condition* will be deleted. For instance, the following statement deletes all male employees:

DELETE FROM EMPLOYEE
WHERE Gender = '*Male*' ;

```
INSERT INTO EMPLOYEE VALUES
(171717171 , 'Debra' , 'Beacon' , '15-Aug-1961' , 'Female' , 70000 , 15 , 'Baron Hill' , 'Calgary' ,
'T2X Y0Y' , 1) ;
INSERT INTO EMPLOYEE VALUES
(181817178 , 'Sam' , 'Field' , '17-Feb-1978' , 'Male' , 40000 , 15 , 'Kick Way' , 'Calgary' , 'Y2K K0K' ,
1) ;
INSERT INTO EMPLOYEE VALUES
(123456789 , 'Rajeet' , 'Folk' , '30-Apr-1967' , 'Male' , 78000 , 123 , 'One Road' , 'Toronto' , 'H1H J9J'
, 2) ;
INSERT INTO EMPLOYEE VALUES
(987654321 , 'Marie' , 'Band' , '12-Jan-1985' , 'Female' , 53500 , 2828 , 'Exit Close' , 'Toronto' ,
'K8O O8K' , 2) ;
INSERT INTO EMPLOYEE VALUES
(666333999 , 'Saleh' , 'Dice' , '25-Mar-1970' , 'Male' , 90400 , 66 , 'Straight Way' , 'Toronto' , 'T4E T6B'
, 1) ;

INSERT INTO DEPARTMENT VALUES (1 , 'IT' , 171717171 , '12-Feb-2008') ;
INSERT INTO DEPARTMENT VALUES (2 , 'Finance' , 123456789 , '1-Mar-2002') ;
INSERT INTO DEPARTMENT VALUES (3 , 'Marketing' , 666333999 , '1-Jan-2005') ;

INSERT INTO PROJECT VALUES (1 , 'Web Shopping' , 'Calgary' , 1) ;
INSERT INTO PROJECT VALUES (2 , 'Network Upgrade' , 'Calgary' , 1) ;
INSERT INTO PROJECT VALUES (2 , 'New Benefits' , 'Toronto' , 3) ;
INSERT INTO PROJECT VALUES (4 , 'Product XT345' , 'Toronto' , 3) ;

INSERT INTO PROJ_EMP VALUES (171717171 , 1 , 15) ;
INSERT INTO PROJ_EMP VALUES (171717171 , 2 , 20) ;
INSERT INTO PROJ_EMP VALUES (171717171 , 3 , 5) ;
INSERT INTO PROJ_EMP VALUES (181817178 , 1 , 30) ;
INSERT INTO PROJ_EMP VALUES (181817178 , 2 , 10) ;
INSERT INTO PROJ_EMP VALUES (123456789 , 3 , 40) ;
INSERT INTO PROJ_EMP VALUES (666333999 , 4 , 40) ;
```

Figure 4.13: Populating the database of Figure 4.1

Exercises

1. Design a simple university ERD:

    • The university has students, courses, and instructors

    • The database will be used to keep track of student completion of courses and the respective final letter grades

    • We should be able to tell which instructor taught a given student and in what course

2. Design an ERD for criminal records. Data should be kept about offenders, offenses, and court trials.

3. Design a music library ERD. The library has all kinds of records (disks, phonographs, etc.). For each song/instrumental, the library keeps track of all musicians who participated in making the song/instrumental (who did what: vocal, piano, drums, lyrics, composing, etc.). It also keeps track of duration, date, and other properties of each song/instrumental.

4. Map the ERD of the previous questions to a database schema.

5. How would you handle the relationship-type PLAYS of Figure 4.8 in Section 4.3 when mapping the ERD to a schema?

6. The ERD of Figure 4.8 in Section 4.3 does not record details such as which player scored, assisted in a score, was injured, or was suspended. It also does not record the match referees. Modify the ERD to capture such details.

7. On the sample database of Figure 4.1, write the following queries in SQL and QBE (where possible):

    (a) Retrieve employees whose salary is less than 30K.

    (b) Retrieve employees whose salary is less than 30K and live in Toronto.

    (c) Retrieve employees whose salary is more than 30K or do not live in Toronto .

    (d) Retrieve projects that are controlled by the Finance department.

    (e) (challenging) Retrieve the departments that control at least one project and are managed by a female employee.

    (f) Find the total number of hours each employee is working on projects.

    (g) Find the average hours that employees are working on each project.

    (h) Find the total salary per department, as long as the total is more than 100K.

    (i) (very challenging) Find the employees who work on all the projects that are controlled by the IT department.

8. Map the ERD of Figure 4.6 in Section 4.3 to a schema. Then write the following queries in SQL:

   (a) Find all the books that correspond to courses in Fall 2010.

   (b) Find the sellers who currently have active books for sale and who have a rating of more than 9.

9. Map the ERD of Figure 4.7 in Section 4.3 to a schema. Create the schema in Microsoft Access, and formulate the following queries in QBE:

   (a) Find all the songs by Michael Jackson.

   (b) Find each album that contains at least one song by Michael Jackson and at least one song by Jennifer Lopez.

10. Map the ERD of Figure 4.9 in Section 4.3 to a schema. Create the schema in Microsoft Access, and formulate the following queries in SQL or QBE:

   (a) Find the species of the trees that were measured in 1998.

   (b) Find the species of the trees that are in forests above 1600m in altitude.

   (c) Find the employees who took measurements on pine trees.

   (d) (very challenging) Find the trees that had all their measurements performed before 2001 and these trees are located in forests that are at least 10KM in area.

CHAPTER 5

Making Computers Think: Programming

Machines, including computers, solve problems by transforming an input into an output. A washing machine solves the "laundry problem" by transforming dirty clothes, the input, into clean clothes, the output. Unlike other machines, computers are versatile: they can be *programmed* to solve almost any problem.

Computer *programs* are specific step-by-step instructions that outline how to convert some input to appropriate output. That is, programs are concrete implementations of algorithms, using a specific programming language. The language that will be studied in this chapter is called *Alice*. It was created for an educational purpose, is used to create 3D animations, and can be a lot of fun.

Examples in this chapter are supported by "how to" movies. Each is supplemented by a starter file, that you should use to do the exercise yourself, and a result file, which shows you how your program should look like after performing the exercise. These movies, along with the required files are available at:

`http://pages.cpsc.ucalgary.ca/~kawash/peeking/alice-how-to.html`

In this chapter, we use the following font conventions:

Font	Used for
COMP	COMP is a component in the Alice environment
input	input is an input element in the Alice environment, such as a button
var	*var* is a variable name
meth	*meth* is a method name
obj.*meth*	*meth* is a method in object *obj*
Stmt	Stmt is an Alice programming structure or statement

141

5.1   Algorithms & Programs

Algorithms can be specified in different ways: from pseudo-code to programs. Here, we focus on how to implement algorithms using programs.

Computers only understand 0s and 1s, and this language of 0s and 1s is called *machine language*. Programming in machine language is too difficult if not impossible. Instead, programmers write their programs in a *high-level* (HL) programming language. It is much easier to program using HL languages since they allow us to write a program using English-like instructions, and they are formal enough to be converted to machine language or *low-level* (LL) code. Different machines may have different LL languages, depending on the way they are built.

The conversion from HL to LL programs is called *translation*. Translators are programs that perform this conversion. The input to a translator is a HL program, and the output is a LL program that is equivalent to the HL program. There are two types of translation methods: *compilation* and *interpretation*. Both convert HL code to LL code, but they do it differently. Compilers read the whole HL program and translate it entirely to a LL program before the LL program is executed. Interpreters read one HL instruction at a time, translate it to LL, and execute it. There are advantages and disadvantages for each translation method, which will not be discussed here. Some programming languages, such as Java, use a combination of compilation and interpretation.

Programming languages (HL or LL) have grammatical rules that need to be followed. Programs follow grammatical rules just like in English or French; each sentence has a particular grammatical structure. The difference is that grammar of programs is very strict and must be followed to the letter for the program to be translated or executed. The grammar of a language is called *syntax*, and the meaning of a program (or a sentence in the case of natural languages) is referred to as *semantics*.

In what follows, we will study the basic parts of speech of a simple programming language called Alice. Alice is an *object-oriented* language, and the concept of an *object* plays a central role in such languages. Learning a programming language is similar to learning the grammar of natural languages. You have to know the grammar of the language and its vocabulary before using it. A fundamental difference is that programming languages are used by computers; thus to speak computer languages, you have to train yourself to think like a computer.

5.2   The Alice Environment

Figure 5.1 shows the basic Alice environment. The WORLD VIEW window shows the background and the objects added to the scene. The OBJECT TREE window lists all the objects in the scene. The OBJECT DETAILS window shows the details (properties, methods, and functions in three tabs) of a selected object. An object can be selected by either clicking on it in the OBJECT TREE window or in the WORLD VIEW. In Figure 5.1, *cow* is selected in the OBJECT TREE window, and the OBJECT DETAILS window lists the methods *cow*.*move*, *cow*.*turn*, *cow*.*roll*, etc. The METHOD EDITOR is where methods are created. At the bottom of the METHOD EDITOR is the STATEMENT BAR, which includes various Alice statements that can be added to a method by dragging and dropping them into the METHOD EDITOR. We will not discuss the EVENT EDITOR in this book.

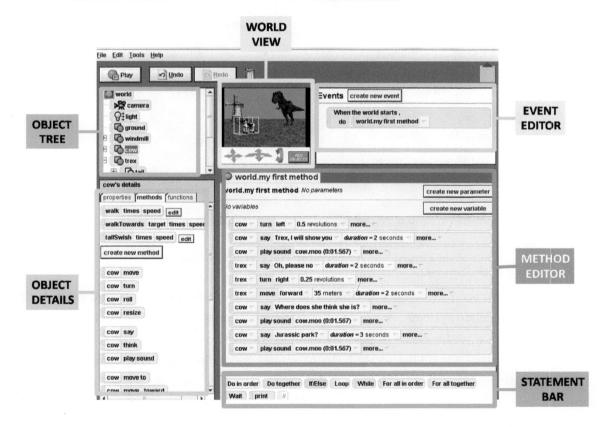

Figure 5.1: The Alice environment

5.3   Objects & Classes

An Alice program is called a *virtual world* or simply a *world*, and it implements an animated movie or game. A world is a collection of *objects*. All characters and props in a world are objects. Figure 5.2 shows a world with the three objects: a **windmill**, a **trex** (Tyrannosaurus Rex)) dinosaur, and a **cow**. In fact, the world itself is also an object, as shall be seen later in the chapter.

Figure 5.2: An example Alice virtual world

An object is an *instance* of a class. Objects and classes are respectively similar to entities and entity-types in database systems. A *class* is a type, template, or blue print. For instance, Cow[1] is a class, describing a set (or class) of possibly many cows. All cows have similar features, called *properties*. Properties are similar to attributes of entities and entity-types. For example, all cow objects have the properties: color, length, and weight. Note that here, we are not referring to a particular cow, your cow, my cow, or your neighbor's cow. When we talk about the neighbors cow, we are talking about a specific cow object, an instance of the Cow class. Now we can say for example that the neighbor's cow is brown, is 2 meters long, and weighs 150 kg. Hence, these common properties between Cow objects can be given different values for different objects.

A class defines the common properties for its instances. For example, a cow object would have the properties: color and size. Though any cow object must have at least these two properties, different cow objects may have different values for these properties. One cow can be brown, and

---

[1]we will always capitalize the initial letter of a class name.

the other can be white; they may also have different sizes.

Figure 5.3: Three instances (objects) of the Cow class

The cow object in Figure 5.2 is an instance of the Alice class Cow. We can create (or instantiate) several cow objects from the same blueprint, the Cow class. Figure 5.3 shows three similar but not identical cows. The object *cow1* is red in color, and the object *cow3* is blue. The objects also do not necessarily have the same size; *cow2* is twice as large as *cow1* and *cow3*. Yet, all of these objects exhibit common behavior: all can move and talk, for instance.

A class also specifies the common *behavior* of its object instances. The behavior of objects is specified by the class as a collection of *methods*. A method is a small program that can be executed when you run an Alice world. One possible method for a cow object is the *move* method, which allows the *cow* to move from one place to another. Methods can also change the properties of an object. Perhaps the best way to change the value of a property of an object is to use a method. Figure 5.4 shows the various methods for a cow object and demonstrates how to change the color of the cow object.

To change an object's property using a method, right-click on the object and select methods. For instance, right-clicking on the cow object, choosing the method *cow set color to*, and then choosing the *magenta* color will change the cow's color to magenta.

Figure 5.4: Cow methods

Example 5.1

Before creating a program in Alice, the initial scene must be set. An appropriate background must be selected and the various objects (characters and props) must be added to the scene. The following steps illustrate how to create the scene in Figure 5.2.

1. Start Alice, and make sure the "Templates" tab is selected in the welcome window:

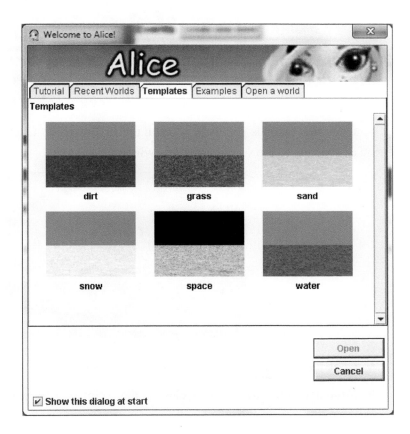

2. Click the grass background and press Open .

3. Click the ADD OBJECTS button in the WORLD VIEW window. The class gallery will appear:

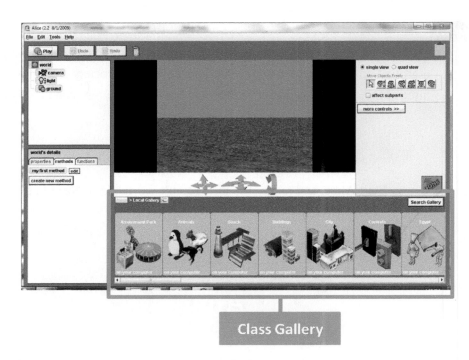

Class Gallery

4. Click the Animals gallery, and scroll to the Cow class. Click the Cow class to add a cow object to the scene. The class window appears:

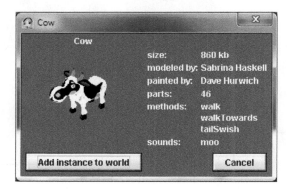

5. Click [Add instance to world]. An instance of Cow is added on the grass background.

6. Similarly, scroll for the Trex class in the Animals gallery, and add a Trex object to the scene.

7. Navigate back to the "Local Galleries", and choose the Buildings gallery. Scroll for the Windmill class, and add an instance of it.

8. Click the green [DONE] button above the top right corner of the class gallery.

9. Adjust the positions of these objects in the scene as desired by dragging them around with the mouse in the WORLD VIEW window.

Each object has a *bounding box*, *center point*, and the relative directions: *forward*, *right*, and *up*. Figure 5.5 shows these features with an example *cow* object. The forward direction is shown as a blue line. So, if you call the method ***cow**.move(forward)*, it moves in the direction of this blue line. Similarly, *up* is shown in green and *right* in red. The point at which all these lines intersect is the center point for this *cow* object. Finally, the bounding box is drawn in yellow. To bring out the bounding box, click an object in the world view window.

Figure 5.5: The bounding box

An object can consist of other objects. This is called *object composition*. The OBJECT TREE window shows the composition of objects in a tree structure. Under each object, it lists the objects that this object is composed of. Figure 5.6 shows a partial tree for *cow* in the OBJECT TREE window. For instance, under *cow* you will find *body* and *neck*, and under *body* there are three objects: *back*, *frontRightThigh*, and *frontleftThigh*. These objects are further composed of other objects.

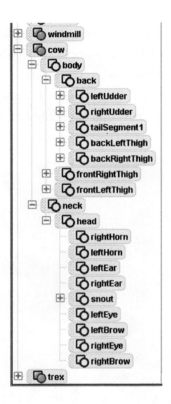

Figure 5.6: Composition of the *cow* object

5.4   Alice Programs

As we mentioned earlier, a method is a small program that instructs an object to behave in a certain way. The method ***world***.*my first method* is the main program of an Alice animation. When the [🖲 Play] button (above OBJECT TREE) is pressed, the program gets translated to LL code, and ***world***.*my first method* is executed. It gets executed when the world starts. Before we develop a program in the ***world***.*my first method*, the program must first be designed. In Alice, the design is called *a storyline*.

Example 5.2 ──

Let's start with a simple storyline and then create it in ***world***.*my first method*.

> *In an open field with a **windmill** in the background,*
> *a **trex** approaches a **cow** from behind;*
> *the **cow** turns towards the **trex**, says "Trex, I will show you" and moos;*
> *the frightened **trex**, says "Oh please no", turns towards the **windmill**, and*
> *runs away, until she disappears from the scene;*
> *the triumphant **cow** says "Where does she think she is", moos, continues*
> *"Jurassic Park?", and moos again in celebration.*

Once, the initial scene is set, the program is created by repeating the following steps:

1. Decide which object is performing an action next, and select this object in the OBJECT TREE or the WORLD VIEW window.

2. Choose an appropriate method from the OBJECT DETAILS window, drag and drop it into the METHOD EDITOR, and specify any required parameters.

The result is the program in Figure 5.7. First, the *cow* turns to the left half a revolution so that it is facing the trex. That is, `cow  turn left  0.5 revolutions  more...`. Then, the *cow* says "Trex, I will show you". The call-out lasts for two seconds. That is, `cow  say Trex, I will show you  duration = 2 seconds  more...`. The *cow* then plays the sound "moo", or `cow  play sound cow.moo (0:01.567)  more...`. The rest of the method should be easily understood.

 The movie *cow-trex-1* shows you how to create this program.

Starter file: No starter file is required.

Result file: `cow-trex1.a2w`

Figure 5.7: The `Cow-Trex` program

5.4.1   Variables

Often programs operate on data, which must be stored in the computer's memory. Programs use symbolic names in order to refer to locations in memory. These symbolic names are called *variables*. Variables have types that specify which range of values can be stored in these variables. The most commonly used variable types in Alice are *number*, *Boolean*, *object*, and *string*. Number variables can be used to store any number. Boolean variables can store one of two values: **true** or **false**. Object variables are used to refer to objects, such as *cow* and *trex*. String variables are used to store text values. There are many other variable types under the "other" radio button (Figure 5.9). Figure 5.8 shows four different variable types and their representation in Alice.

Variable *x* is of type number, as indicated by the "123" icon. Variable *y* is of type Boolean, as indicated by the "T/F" icon. Variable *z* is of type object, as indicated by the "Obj" icon. Variable *s* is of type string, as indicated by the "ABC" icon.

Figure 5.8: Four variables in Alice

Object properties, such as *color*, are also variables. To add a new property to an object, click the create new variable button in the OBJECT DETAIL window. The window shown in Figure 5.9 will appear. Specify the variable name, type, and initial value. Variables can be also created in methods; such objects are called *local variables*. Unlike properties, such variables are local to the method and can only be used inside the method in which they are defined. To create a local variable, click the create new variable button in the METHOD EDITOR ; the same window shown in Figure 5.9 will appear.

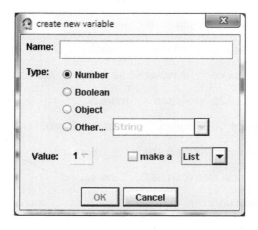

Figure 5.9: Creating a new variable

Variables can be assigned values by using an *assignment statement*. If *x* is a number variable, the statement:

$$x = 12$$

is read "x is assigned the value 12". The effect of an assignment statement is that the value 12 is stored in the memory location referred to by x. From this point on in the program, when x is used, it is substituted by its value. For instance the statement:

cow.*jump(up,x)*

causes the ***cow*** to jump up 12 meters, given that the value stored in x is 12. We will use '=' to represent assignment statements in our pseudo-code and storylines. In Alice, an assignment statement is represented by:

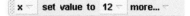

To change the value of a variable in Alice, drag the variable into the METHOD EDITOR. Alice gives options for the assigned value as shown in Figure 5.10. Choosing "set value", gives you some options for a value, such as **0.25**, **0.5**, **1**, and **2**. If you require a value other than those specified in the list, choose "other", and enter the required value.

We will come across assignment statements in many examples later in the chapter.

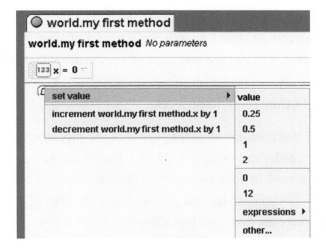

Figure 5.10: Options for assigning a value to a variable

The method editor also has a create new parameter button. *Parameters* are similar to local variables in that they can only used as variables inside their method. Unlike local variables, however, parameters must be given values when the method or function is called. For instance, when calling the ***trex***.*turn*, the method requires the parameter ***direction*** to be initialized to, say, right or left. The *turn* method has other parameters, such as ***revolutions*** and ***duration***. We will see examples of creating your own method with its parameters later in the chapter.

5.4.2   Some useful Alice statements

Printing

Often, a programs contain errors and mistakes, called *bugs*. The process of finding these bugs is called *debugging*. One tool you can use to debug a program is to include statements that instruct the program to *print* variable values or specific messages. In Alice, this can be achieved by the `Print` statement. When `Print` is dragged and dropped into the `METHOD EDITOR`, Alice gives the option of printing a *text string* or an *object*. A text string is printed as is, but for an object, its value is printed. When a world is played, the effect of `Print` statements is shown at the bottom of the "play" window.

Program comments

Programs can become large and hard to understand. Hence, it is beneficial to *document* your program. This can be achieved by the comment `//` statement. These comments are ignored by Alice when the world is played, but are included to explain the program and can provide other information, such as the name of the program creator and the date of creation.

Waiting

The `Wait` statement instructs an object to wait for a period of time before proceeding with the following statement. That is, it delays the execution of the statement that follows the `Wait`.

5.4.3   The *world* and other built-in objects

Alice *world* is an object that contains all other objects in the program. Just like any other object, *world* has properties, methods, and functions. In fact, this object has a large amount of methods and functions that can be used in your programs. Click on the *world* object in the `OBJECT TREE` window, and explore the `OBJECT DETAILS` to get familiar with some of the available methods and functions. In particular, there are functions that allow you to collect user input and to perform logic operations, calculations, and comparisons.

In addition to the *world* object, any Alice world has the objects *camera*, *light*, and *ground*. These objects contain many methods and functions that can be useful in your programs. Explore these objects in the `OBJECT TREE` and `OBJECT DETAILS` to learn about their methods and functions.

5.4.4   Methods and functions

Methods define object behavior. Functions are special kinds of methods: they return values. Unlike regular methods, functions must be used as a substitution for parameters or as an assigned value to a variable. The value a function returns substitutes the parameter or is assigned to the variable.

Example 5.3 ———

To create a new method:

1. In the OBJECT TREE (or the WORLD VIEW) window, click on the object to which the method is going to be added.

2. Make sure the "methods" tab is selected in the OBJECT DETAILS window.

3. In the "methods" tab, click create new method .

4. A window will pop up asking for the method name; enter the method name and click OK .

5. If the method requires parameters, click create new parameter in the METHOD EDITOR . Specify the name and type of the parameter, just like any other variable (as in Figure 5.9). Repeat these steps if more parameters are needed.

6. The method program can now be constructed just like we constructed *world*.*my first method* earlier.

Creating a function is similar. Make sure the functions tab is selected in the OBJECT DETAILS window, and click create new function . Note, however, that a function must have a Return statement, which is inserted by default into the function's body.

5.5 Control Flow

The `Cow-Trex` program shown in Figure 5.7 is *straight-line* code: the statements are executed in sequence, one after another. However, programs may need to have two methods executed at the same time, such as having *trex* move her legs and tail while she is moving forward. This creates a more realistic "walking" movement.

5.5.1 Doing in order and together

All the method calls of the `Cow-Trex` program of Figure 5.7 are executed *in order*. The *cow*.*turn* method is executed until completion before the following method, *cow*.*say*, is called. Once the *cow*.*turn* is completed, *cow*.*say* is executed, and so on. This results in a straight-line flow of the execution of methods.

However, the animation would be more realistic if we allow some of these methods to be executed concurrently, or in parallel. For instance, *cow* can say "Trex, I will show you", while a moo sound is playing. This can be achieved by the *do together* Alice statement. The Do in order and Do together statements simply enclose other statements and method calls. The statements that are in a Do in order statement are executed one after another. Those that are in a Do together statement are executed in parallel.

Example 5.4

To use the Do in order or Do together statements, drag the statement from the STATEMENT BAR ,
and drop it into the METHOD EDITOR . Then, add to it any other statements and method
calls. Next, we revise the *Cow-Trex* movie to include these statements.

Figure 5.11 shows the revised story line of our *Cow-Trex* movie. First, note that the
windmill rolls its **blades** throughout the scene. That is, this is *done together* with the rest
of the story events. The methods **cow**.*turn*, **cow**.*say*, **cow**.*moo*, **trex**.*say*, and **trex**.*turn* are
all done *in order* as indicated by the flow arrows in Figure 5.11. Following the **trex**.*turn*
method, two methods are executed *together*; these are **trex**.*run* and **cow.head**.*turn*. Both
are completed before the following method, **cow**.*says*, begins. The resulting program is
shown in Figure 5.12.

 The movie *cow-trex-2* shows you how to create this program.

Starter file: `cow-trex1.a2w`

Result file: `cow-trex2.a2w`

Note in Figure 5.12 how these statements can be nested: a Do in order or Do together statement
can include other Do in order or Do together statements.

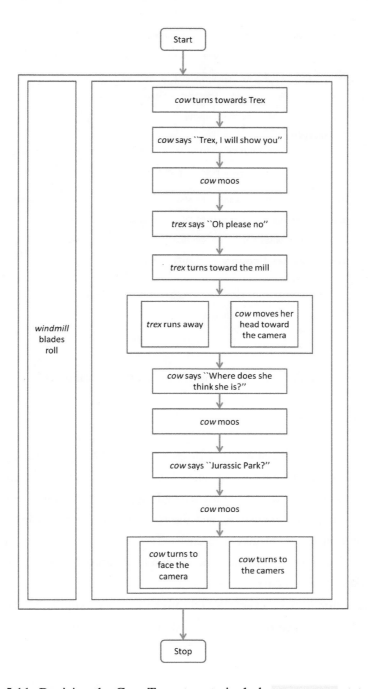

Figure 5.11: Revising the Cow-Trex story to include do together statements

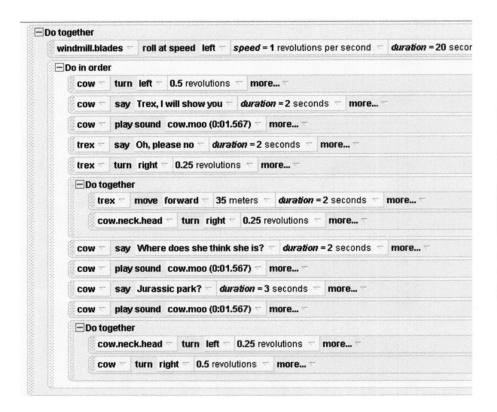

Figure 5.12: Program for the story in Figure 5.11

5.5.2   Conditionals

Often programs need to make decisions. The program of an ATM checks to see if you have enough money in the account before dispensing any cash. If you have enough money to make a withdrawal, the ATM still needs to verify that you are not exceeding your daily limit. Hence, the output of the ATM depends on making some decisions, and the result could be dispensing cash or displaying a message telling you that it cannot give you cash. This kind of execution is called *branching* or *conditional execution*, and the statements that allow a program to behave in such a way are called *branching* or *conditional statements*.

Conditional execution in Alice is achieved through the If/Else statement. These statements have *If* and *Else* parts. The general form of an If/Else statement is as follows:

 If *if-condition*

  if-body

 Else

  else-body

The *if-condition* is a Boolean expression (a proposition) that is either **true** or **false**. An If/Else statement is executed as follows. First, the *if-condition* is tested: if it is **true**, the *if-body* is executed but the *else-body* is skipped. If the *if-condition* is **false**, the *if-body* will be skipped, but the *else-body* will be executed. In either case, execution continues with the statement that immediately follows the If/Else statement.

Flowcharts

A flowchart is a visual representation of the program flow. The storyline diagram depicted in Figure 5.11 is a flowchart. The flowcharts that we use here are very simple. Boxes indicate statements that do not involve decisions, such as method calls or assignment statements. We use a diamond shape to indicate a branching decision, with two possible outcomes, either **true** or **false**. The flow of an If/Else statement is depicted in Figure 5.13.

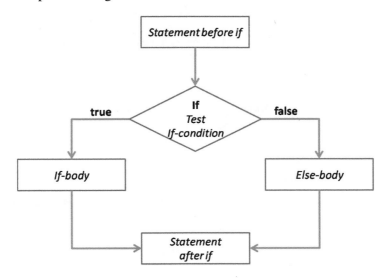

Figure 5.13: Flowchart of an If/Else statement

Example 5.5

To use the If/Else statement, drag the statement from the STATEMENT BAR , and drop it into the METHOD EDITOR . This requires you to specify the *if-condition*. Choose **true** for now. Once you decide on the Boolean functions required for the *if-condition*, drag the function, and drop it to replace **true**. Finally, add any other statements and method calls to the *if-body* or *else-body*.

Let's illustrate If/Else statements through an example, with the following storyline. A monkey in a desert is desperate to get to an oasis. He stumbles across a stop sign protected by a ghost. The ghost tells the monkey that he can get to the oasis only if he can jump higher than the stop sign. Otherwise, the monkey will be captured by the ghost. The monkey accepts the deal, and he tries the jump. To make the program interesting, we will make the monkey jump a *random* number of meters. That is, we do not specify the height value. We let it have a random value that can be different every time we play the world. Then, we assess the height of his jump. If the jump is higher than the stop sign, the monkey will go to the oasis. If not, the monkey will be captured by the ghost.

The flowchart for this story line is as follows:

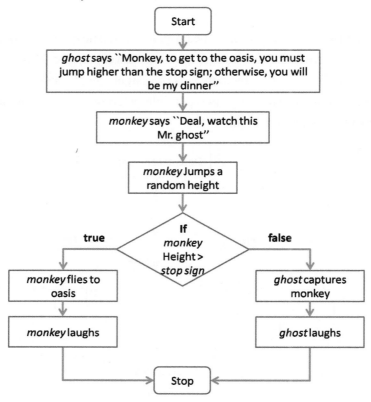

The program is in Figure 5.14.

 The movie *monkey-ghost* shows you how to create this program.

Starter file: `monkey-ghost-starter.a2w`

Result file: `monkey-ghost.a2w`

If/Else statements can be nested. The *if-body* or the *else-body* can include other If/Else statements.

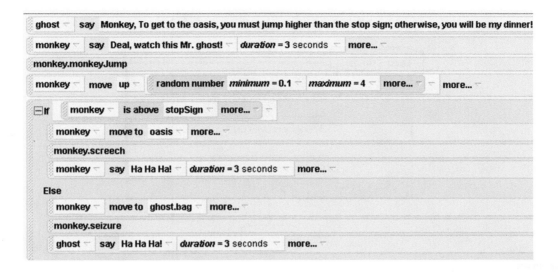

Figure 5.14: The *Monkey-Ghost* program

5.5.3 Loops

Loops are programming structures that allow a program segment to be repeated as many times as required. Alice has two types of loops: Loop and While. The Loop statement is suitable for a program segment to be repeated a fixed number of times, such as making the ***monkey*** jump five times. The While statement is used when a segment is repeated until a Boolean condition is met, such as making the ***monkey*** keep jumping until he is higher than the ***stop sign***.

Loop

The Loop statement allows a segment to be repeated a specific number of times. The following is a program where the ***monkey*** jumps five times:

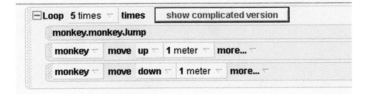

That is, the sequence of method calls ***monkey***.*jump*, ***monkey***.*move(up)*, and ***monkey***.*move(down)* is repeated five times. This program is captured by the flowchart:

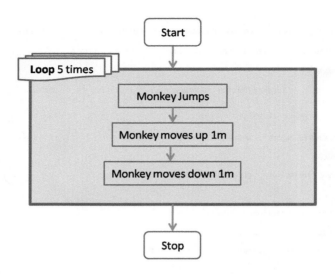

Example 5.6

To use the Loop statement, drag the statement from the STATEMENT BAR , and drop it into
the METHOD EDITOR . Then, add any other statements and method calls to its body.

The *Cow-Trex* program of Figure 5.12 shows **trex** running away from the **cow** without
moving her legs or tail. We will write a new *walk* method for **trex**, making use of the
 Loop statement in order to make her movement more realistic. The method is given in
Figure 5.15. There are two Loop statements that are *done together*. The first requires the
trex.leftThigh to move forward, followed by a forward movement of ***trex.rightThigh***.
Then both thighs move backwards. This simulates walking. The loop is repeated two
times, which is sufficient before **trex** disappears from the scene. The second Loop is
repeated five times, and it moves ***trex.tail*** up and down, while she is walking, adding to
the realistic appearance of her walk.

 The movie *cow-trex-3* shows you how to create this program.

Starter file: `cow-trex2.a2w`

Result file: `cow-trex3.a2w`

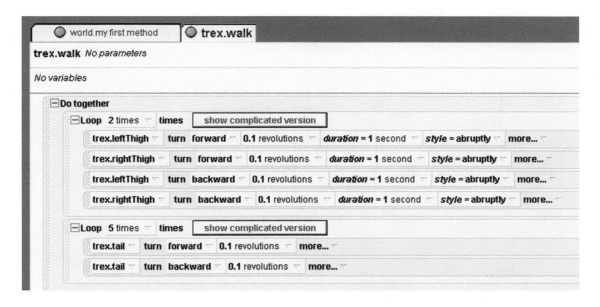

Figure 5.15: The *trex.walk* method

While

The While statement is a combination of If/Else and Loop statements. It has the following general structure:

> While *while-condition*
>   *while-body*

Similar to an If/Else statement, the *while-condition* is a Boolean condition. The execution of a While statement starts by checking the *while-condition*. If it is **true**, the *while-body* is executed. Unlike an If/Else statement, (1) the While has no *Else* part, and (2) *while-body* can be executed several times. In fact, the *while-body* is executed as long as *while-condition* is **true**. Before the beginning of every iteration, the *while-condition* is checked, and the loop keeps iterating until the condition becomes **false**. The flowchart in Figure 5.16 explains the While statement operation.

Example 5.7 _____

To use the While statement, drag the statement from the STATEMENT BAR , and drop it into the METHOD EDITOR . This requires you to specify the *while-condition*. Choose **true** for now. Once you decide on the Boolean functions required for the *while-condition*, drag the function, and drop it to replace **true**. Then add any other statements and method calls to the *while-body*.

We illustrate the use of *While* loops in this example. A ***rescue helicopter*** approaches a ***lifeboat*** and hovers over it, dropping down until it gets close to it. The storyline can be described using the following pseudo-code:

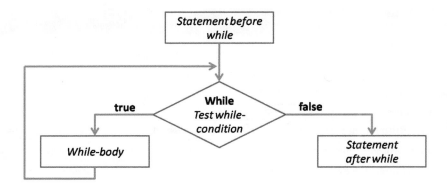

Figure 5.16: Flowchart for While statement

Do together

   helicopter.*heli blade*

    Do inorder

      helicopter *turns its face to the* **lifeboat**

      helicopter *moves forward until it is above the* **lifeboat**

      While **helicopter** *is more than 1/2 meters above the* **lifeboat**

        helicopter *drops down 1/2 meter*

The program is as follows:

```
⊟Do together
   helicopter.heli blade
   ⊟Do in order
      helicopter ⌄   turn to face  lifeBoat ⌄   more... ⌄
      helicopter ⌄   move  forward ⌄   (  helicopter ⌄   distance to  lifeBoat.rowPerson.head ⌄  ⌄  . 1 ⌄  )  ⌄
      ⊟While   helicopter ⌄   distance above  lifeBoat ⌄   more... ⌄  ⌄   > 0.5 ⌄  ⌄
         helicopter ⌄   move  down ⌄   0.5 meters ⌄   more... ⌄
```

The method **helicopter**.*heli blade* uses *infinite* loops to rotate the **helicopter** blades. A While statement with the *while-condition* set to **true** is an example of an infinite loop. The **helicopter**.*move(forward)* method makes use of the function **helicopter**.*distance to* to calculate the distance from the **helicopter** to an appropriate point in the **lifeboat**. Note that to center the **helicopter** on top of the **lifeboat**, we chose to move it above the row person's head minus one meter. Once the **helicopter** is positioned above the **lifeboat**, the While statement drops it 1/2 meter (**helicopter**.*move(down)*) until the *while-condition* is **false**, that is, until the **helicopter**.*distance above(lifeboat)* ≤ 0.5.

The movie *helicopter-boat* shows you how to create this program.

Starter file: No starter file is required.

Result file: `helicopter-boat.a2w`

5.6 Lists

A *list* variable bundles a collection of variables together. Formally, a list is a tuple of values. The order of the list items is specified by an *index* for each item. The first item on the list is at index 0, the second is at index 1, and so on. The following is a conceptual view of a list of five names:

In this list, John is at index 0, Frank at index 1, and so on.

Example 5.8

Lists are created as variables. To make a variable a list, check the ⌐make a list⌐ box in the "new variable" window (Figure 5.9). Alice expands the window to allow you to populate the list:

Note that in this example, we have chosen the list ***spaceTeam*** to be a list of objects. To add an object to the list, click ⌐new item⌐:

Item 0 in the list is still not assigned a value, as indicated by <None>. To assign a value to item 0, click <None>. Alice will show you a list of the available objects in the world:

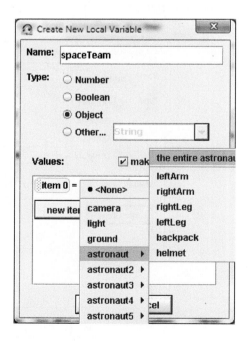

The process of creating new items must be repeated to add another item to the list. For instance, the following is a list of 4 astronaut objects:

The statements For all in order and For all together are specific to lists. The For all in order state-ment applies the body of the statement to each item on the list starting at index 0, incrementing the index by 1 after each iteration. The For all together statement asks the items on the list to all do something at the same time (together). Let *list* be a list variable to which For all in order or For all together is applied. Let the size of *list* be n. Recall that *list[i]* denotes the ith item of *list*. Figure 5.17 explains the operation of:

 For all in order (respectively, For all together) applied to *list*

    for-all-body

Although For all in order and For all together can be expressed in flowcharts using the While and Do together statements, we will shortly introduce simpler flowchart symbols specific to these for all statements.

Example 5.9

To use the For all in order or For all together statement, drag the statement from the STATEMENT BAR , and drop it into the METHOD EDITOR . Alice prompts for an existing list or a new list. For instance, adding a For all in order statement to a method, Alice shows:

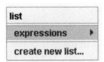

Either create a new list, or choose "expressions" for available (already created) lists:

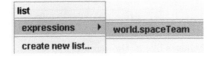

After choosing or creating a list, the For all in order statement looks like:

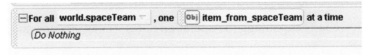

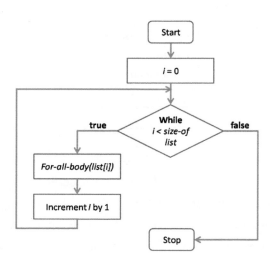

The **For all in order** statement behaves like a **While** statement. The *for-all-body* is applied to each item in the list, in order. In the first iteration of the **While** statement, *i* is 0 and the *for-all-body* is applied to the element at index 0 (*list[0]*). Then *i* is incremented by 1, so that in the second iteration of the **While**, *i* is 1 and the *for-all-body* is applied to *list[1]*. This is repeated until the condition $i < size\text{-}of\ list$ is **false**. That is, it continues until all the items in the list have been considered. Note that if *list* is empty, its size is 0 and the while-condition is **false**, since $0 < 0$ is **false**.

(a)

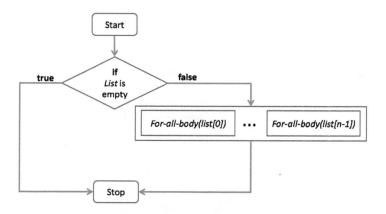

The **For all together** statement behaves like a **Do together** statement. The *for-all-body* is applied to each item in the list, concurrently. That is, the *for-all-body* is applied concurrently to the *n* items of the list *list[0]* to *list[n − 1]*

(b)

Figure 5.17: Flowcharts explaining the operation of (a) **For all in order** and (b) **For all together** statements

The statements in the body of the For all in order or For all together statements should be applied to every item in the given list. Adding a *move* method for a specific object yields:

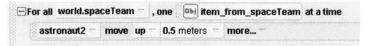

If we leave it as is, the object ***astronaut2*** will be performing the method *move* as many times as the length of the list ***spaceTeam***. This is not what is intended; we want the *move* method to be performed by each item in ***spaceTeam***, not only by ***astronaut2***. To do so, click and choose "expressions" then "item_from_spaceTeam":

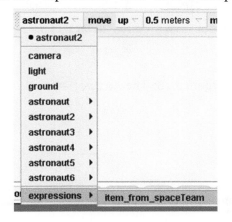

This results in:

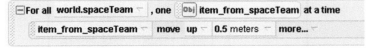

so that the *move* method is applied to each "item_from_spaceTeam" *in order*.

Figure 5.18 shows a program that instructs a list of astronaut objects to perform an acrobatic dance in space. The first statement is a For all in order statement, instructing each astronaut, in turn, to drop on her/his back and then stand up. The second is For all together statement that instructs the ***spaceTeam*** (all at once) to jump up, make a full rotation in space, and go back to the moon surface.

 The movie *astronaut-list* shows you how to create this program.

Starter file: `astronaut-list-start.a2w`

Result file: `astronaut-list.a2w`

A flowchart for the `Astronaut-Dance` program is given in Figure 5.19. The For all in order and For all together are represented similarly to Loop.

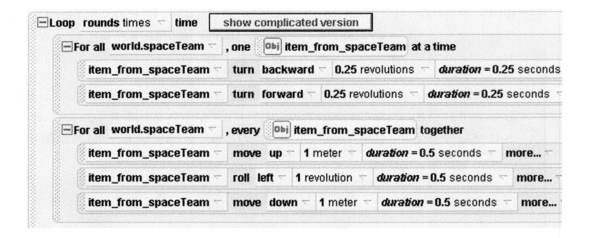

Figure 5.18: The *Astronaut-Dance* program

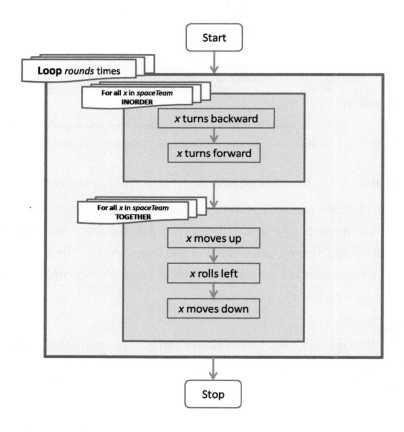

Figure 5.19: Flowchart for the *Astronaut-Dance* program

5.7 Advanced Algorithms

5.7.1 Minimum finding

Recall Algorithm 2.1, which finds the minimum value in a list. A possible Alice implementation of this algorithm is given in figures 5.21 and 5.20. The figure shows that the *min* function is implemented in the **world** object, and it has one parameter: `Obj inputList` , a list of objects. The minimum is determined based on the height of these objects. First, ***min-so-far*** is assigned the value of the first object in ***inputList***, `min-so-far set value to first item from inputList` . Then, the statement `For all inputList , one Obj item_from_inputList at a time` considers every item in ***inputList*** in order. The `If/Else` statement `If subject = item_from_inputList 's height < subject = min-so-far 's height` checks if the height of the given item from ***inputList*** is less than the height of ***min-so-far***. If this is the case, ***min-so-far*** is updated, `min-so-far set value to item_from_inputList` . Note that the *else-body* is left empty. Finally, when the whole list is processed by the for-all statement, ***min-so-far*** is returned.

Note that this implementation differs from Algorithm 2.1 in that the algorithm checks if the input list is empty, but our implementation does not. That modification is left as an exercise.

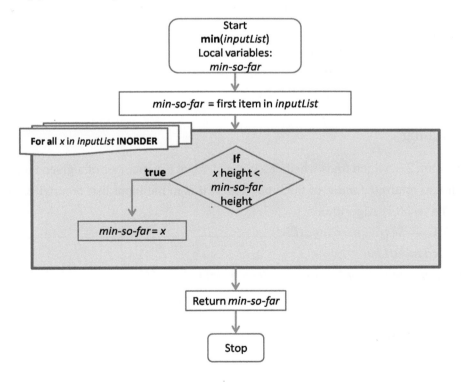

Figure 5.20: Flowchart height-based *min* function in Alice

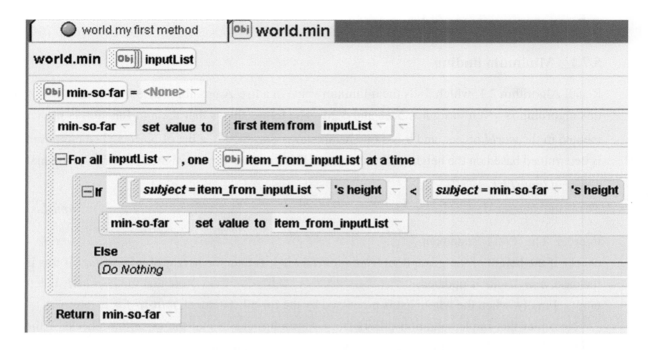

Figure 5.21: Height-based *min* function in Alice

 The movie *astronaut-min* shows you how to create this program.

Starter file: `astronaut-list-min-start.a2w`

Result file: `astronaut-list-min.a2w`

5.7.2   Searching

Recall Algorithm 2.2, which finds whether a given element is a member of a given tuple. We extend this algorithm to return the *index* of the input item if it is in the input list; otherwise, the algorithm returns -1. The result is Algorithm 5.1.

Algorithm 5.1. — *Search(**item**,**inputList**)* _____

*Input: **item** and **inputList***

Output: index of item in inputList or −1 if item is not in inputList

$i = 0$

***nextItem** = **inputList**[i]*

Loop   *size-of **inputList** times*

    *If **nextItem** == **item***

        Return   *i (Stop the search)*

    Else

        increment i by 1

Return   −1
_____

Figures 5.22 and 5.23 both show a possible implementation of Algorithm 5.1 in Alice. This figure shows that the *search* function is implemented in the **world** object. It has two parameters: `Obj inputList`, which is a list of objects, and `Obj item`, a single object. The *search* method has two local variables: `123 i = 0`, a number variable initialized to 0, and `Obj nextItem = <None>`, an object variable with no initial value assigned. The program mimics Algorithm 5.1. The `Loop` statement iterates a maximum of the size of **inputList** iterations. The variable **nextItem** is assigned the item at index 0 in the first iteration, `nextItem set value to item i from inputList`. This is the first element in the list. The *if-condition* compares **nextItem** against the parameter **item**. If these two items are equal, the *if-body* returns the value 0. Note that the `Return` statement terminates the `Loop` statement and the *search* function. Otherwise, the *else-body* sets the value of i to $i+1$, incrementing i, `i set value to ( i + 1 )`. Hence, in the second iteration, i is 1 and **item** is checked against the item at index 1. This can be repeated as many times as there are items on **inputList**, where in iteration k the value of i is $k-1$. If the `Loop` statement performs all its iterations without finding **item** in **inputList**, the last statement, `Return -1`, is reached and the function returns -1.

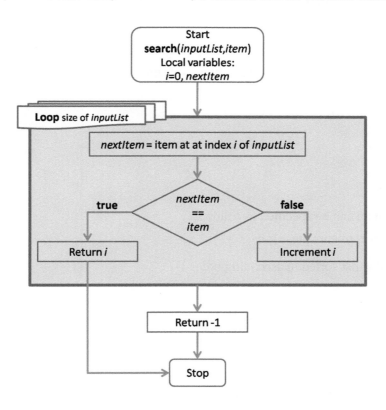

Figure 5.22: Flowchart for sequential *search* function in Alice

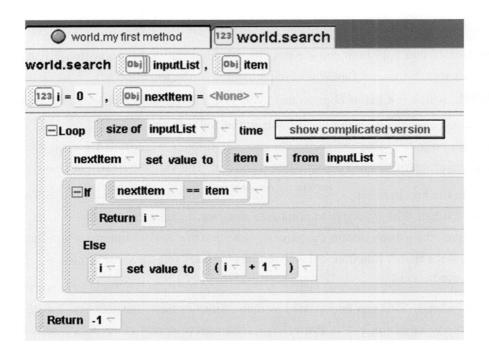

Figure 5.23: Sequential *search* function in Alice

 The movie *astronaut-search* shows you how to create this program.

Starter file: `astronaut-list-min.a2w`

Result file: `astronaut-list-min-search.a2w`

5.7.3   Sorting

The *sorting* problem can be specified as follows:

Input: A list of n elements $[a_0, a_1, a_2, \cdots, a_{n-1}]$

Output: The same list sorted in ascending order

Example 5.10

If the input is $[12, 5, 6, 100, 3, 1]$, the output must be $[1, 3, 5, 6, 12, 100]$.

If the input is [James, Frank, Alicia, Bob, Alice], the output is [Alice, Alicia, Bob, Frank, James].

One known algorithm to sort a list is called *selection sort*. The idea of selection sort is very simple, and we illustrate it through an example first. Given the input $[23, 4, 3, 100]$, we perform 4 iterations, as many elements as we have in the input. In each iteration, we delete the minimum element in the list and append it to a new list, which is initially empty. The algorithm proceeds as follows:

initially old list = $[23, 4, 3, 100]$ and new list $[]$

iteration 1 min = 3, old list = $[23, 4, 100]$, and new list $[3]$

iteration 2 min = 4, old list = $[23, 100]$, and new list $[3, 4]$

iteration 3 min = 23, old list = $[100]$, and new list $[3, 4, 23]$

iteration 4 min = 100, old list = $[]$, and new list $[3, 4, 23, 100]$

Next we specify the selection sort algorithm. This specification illustrates that parameters can be used as output parameters to return values.

Algorithm 5.2. — *Selection-sort(**inputList**,**outputList**)* _____

*Input: **InputList***

*Output: **OutputList***

While ***inputList** is not empty*

      ***minItem** = Min(**inputList**) — this relies on the Min( ) algorithm (Algorithm 2.1)*

      *insert **minItem** at the end of **outputList***

      *remove **minItem** from **inputList***

An implementation of selection-sort is given in figures 5.24 and 5.25. The *While* statement requires the sorting process to stop once ***inputList*** is empty; that is, the *loop* iterates as long as ***inputList*** is non-empty. This is accomplished by using the world *is empty* function and the *not* function, `□While not is inputList empty`. The ***minItem*** variable is assigned the value returned by the ***world**.min* function, developed earlier in this section. After appending ***minItem*** to ***outputList***, it is removed from ***inputList***. To remove an item from a list, the function *remove* requires the index of the item that is to be deleted. For instance, `remove item from position 0 of inputList more...` removes the element at index 0 from ***inputList***. We need to determine the index of ***minItem*** in ***inputList*** before we can delete it from this list. Hence in this program, we are also relying on the ***world**.search* function to return the index of ***minItem*** in ***inputList***, `world.search inputList = inputList item = minItem`. Substituting the returned value of ***world**.search* as a position parameter of the *remove* method, yields: `remove item from position world.search inputList = inputList item = minItem of inputList more...`.

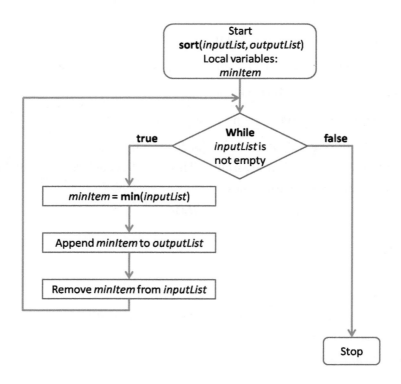

Figure 5.24: Flowchart for election *sort* method in Alice

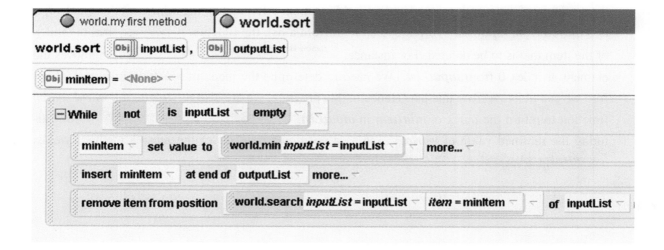

Figure 5.25: Selection *sort* method in Alice

Example 5.11

For the astronauts in *spaceTeam* to board the *lander*, they must first line up, sorted by height:

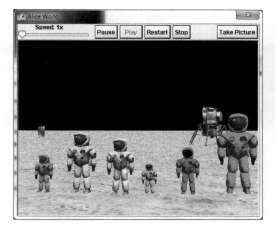
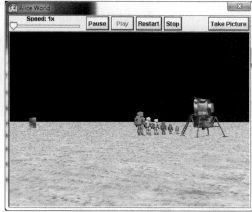

before sorting   after sorting

The program to accomplish this result is:

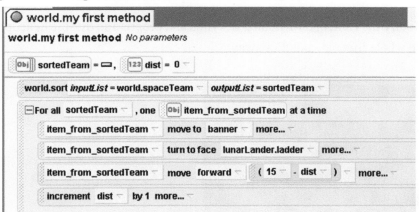

 The movie *astronaut-sort* shows you how to create this program.

Starter file: `astronaut-list-min-search.a2w`

Result file: `astronaut-list-search-sort.a2w`

Exercises

1. Modify the Cow-Trex storyline and program so that the cow follows the trex when running away, jumps on the trex, and pushes her to the ground.

2. Create a flowchart and an Alice program for the following storyline consisting of two penguin objects (Animals Gallery) facing each other. Penguin1 tries to jump over penguin2. The height of the jump is determined randomly. If the penguin1 jumps over penguin2, it lands safely on the ground behind penguin2; otherwise, they both fall down.

3. Modify the Monkey-Ghost storyline and program so that if the ghost captures the monkey, it flies away with the monkey; otherwise, the ghost catches fire (SpecialEffects Gallery) and dies.

4. Write an Alice program that asks the user to enter a number. It then prints POSITIVE if the number is positive, prints NEGATIVE if the number is negative, and prints ZERO otherwise.

5. Create a *hop* method for the Bunny class (Animals Gallery). The method accepts a number parameter that specifies the number of hops the bunny makes.

6. Modify the Helicopter-Lifeboat storyline and program so that the helicopter drops a rope, lifts the whole lifeboat, and flies away.

7. Create an Alice world as follows:

   The Boeing707 object can be found in the Vehicles Gallery. Write an Alice program instructing this jet to crash-land on the water. Use a `While` loop for descending the jet. Use also a `Do together` statement to move the jet forward and downward. After the jet lands and skids on water, follow it with the camera until it stops.

8. Write an Alice function *isSorted*, which accepts a list of numbers as a parameter. The function returns true if the list is sorted and false otherwise. Test the isSorted function in *my first method*.

9. What is the output of the following Alice program?

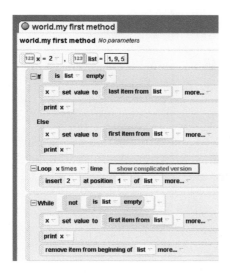

10. Create an Alice program that contains four pj (pajamas) objects (People Gallery):

Group all four pj objects in one list, called wholeTeam; group the two green pj objects in a second list, called greenTeam; group the two blue pj objects in a third list, called blueTeam. Choreograph different dances with this pj team, so that at times the whole team performs the same move, and at other times the greenTeam and blueTeam are performing different moves.

11. Create a *walk* method in the Astronaut class. Modify the program from Example 5.11 so that the astronauts *walk* towards the lander.

12. Create an Alice world with 8 cow objects (Animal Gallery), in which each cow has a different horn size. Use the selection sort algorithm to sort the cows by their horn size.

13. Create flowcharts for storylines of your choice. Create their corresponding Alice programs.

CHAPTER 6

Working Together: Networking & Security

Computers are no longer limited to performing computation. They have become a communication tool. Browsing, instant messaging, voice over IP (VOIP), and media streaming have all become integral parts of our lives. But how do these things work? What happens behind the scenes? Do you still think that the World Wide Web (WWW) and the Internet are the same thing? In this chapter, we will focus on such questions.

This chapter explains what the Internet and the WWW are and what rules computers need to follow so that they communicate with each other. Buzz terms such as TCP/IP, UDP, and HTTP will be explained. In addition, communication cannot be made viable if it is not secure. The types of threats and the security mechanisms that are used to guard against those threats are discussed.

6.1 Networking

You open a browser and type in the address `www.hrw.org`. Suddenly, you see a nicely presented Web page. What actually happened? The page you have just opened was stored on a computer that is located somewhere else, possibly on the other side of the world. The browser, running on your computer, sent a request to the computer that hosts the requested Web page, and that computer sent the Web page to your browser. Let us accept this simplistic view for now, which is depicted in Figure 6.1. Your browser is called the *client program*, and your computer is the *client computer*. The computer that is storing the Web page is called the *server computer*, and there is a program running on it whose job is to serve the client's requests. This program is called the *server program*, or simply the *server*.

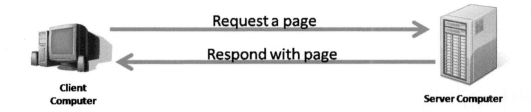

Figure 6.1: Simplified view of client-server interaction

6.1.1 The Internet

For the client and server computers to communicate, they have to be linked through a network. A *network* is a collection of wires, wireless antennas and receivers, satellite connections, and other mechanism that make the two computers communicate. The network infrastructure alone is necessary, but not sufficient, to establish communications. The mere fact that you and your friend have phones is not sufficient for both of you to have a telephone conversation. You need to know how to use the phone, and you and your friend must be able to speak a common language. The rules that make it possible for computers to communicate are called *protocols*. A *networking system* consists of a network and protocols (Figure 6.2). The *Internet* is the largest networking system that ever existed.

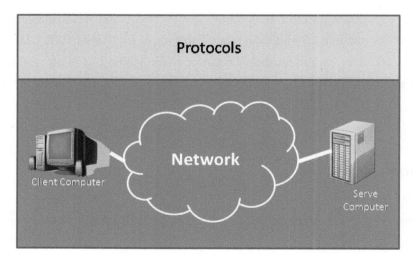

Figure 6.2: The two components of a networking system

Protocols of the Internet

The Internet's protocol suite is called *TCP/IP*. IP stands for *Internet Protocol*, and it mainly specifies an addressing mechanism. Computers need this addressing mechanism to locate one another. The telephone system has an addressing mechanism, which specifies the "addresses" of telephones: country code, area code, and phone number. The postal system also has an addressing mechanism, without which it would be impossible to send post cards and letters to your friends. IP requires that each computer connected to the Internet have a unique *IP address*. The IP address consists of 4 positive integers separated by dots, and each integer must be between 0 and 255. The new version of IP (IPv6) enlarges addresses so that more computers can be connected to the Internet.

Example 6.1

The following are valid IP addresses:

```
150.203.1.2
127.15.30.12
57.83.77.90
```

The following are not valid IP addresses:

```
150.256.1.2
1.2.3.A
150.-1.34.56
```

The address `150.256.1.2` is not valid because 256 is not between 0 and 255. The address `1.2.3.A` is not valid because A is not an integer. The address `150.-1.34.56` is not valid because -1 is not between 0 and 255.

The server computer can have several server programs running on it. It is a large organization, just like your bank branch, where multiple employees with different specialties attend to customers. Typically bank branches have a main telephone number that connects you to the branch, and then you will be asked to dial an extension number to connect to the right person. The IP address is the address of the server computer. To connect to a specific server within the server computer, a client needs an extension number. These extension numbers are called *port numbers*. For instance, Web servers who serve Web pages are typically on port number 80, and email servers use port 25 for sending email messages and port 110 for receiving email messages.

In addition to addressing, the IP protocol is also responsible for routing messages. With the IP addressing mechanism in place, IP is able to find the receiving computer and deliver messages to recipients. We will not dwell on routing here.

The first part of TCP/IP, TCP, stands for *Transmission Control Protocol*. TCP specifies the rules for establishing connections between the client and server computers. These rules are very simple:

1. The server must be listening to some port number, waiting for clients' requests. This port number is the private extension for this server program.

2. A client must request a connection with the desired server, specifying an IP address and a port number. This request is sent from the client computer to the server computer over the

network.

3. The server accepts or rejects the request. If the connection request is accepted, a connection between the client and server is established.

4. The client can send its requests to the server once the connection is established, and the server can send its responses back to the client.

5. Once the client has no further requests, the connection is closed by the client or the server.

A large message is first broken down into smaller equal-sized messages called *packets* or *datagrams*, as depicted in Figure 6.3. These packets are sent separately over the network. They include extra information, such as the addresses of the sender and the receiver and sequential numbers, so that the original message can be re-assembled by the receiving party.

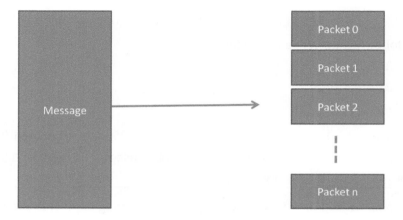

Figure 6.3: Breaking a message into equal-sized packets

TCP is not the only protocol used by the Internet to transport information. The *Universal Datagram Protocol* (UDP) is also part of the Internet protocol suite.

While TCP requires establishing a connection before exchanging messages, UDP does not. This makes TCP a *connection-oriented* protocol and UPD a *connectionless* protocol. The telephone system is a connection-oriented system. To talk to your friend, you have to establish a connection first: you have to dial your friend's number, and she must pick up. The postal system is connectionless. To send your parents a postcard, you do not have to have a connection established ahead of time. You simply address the post card, affix a stamp on it, and drop it in the post office or a postal drop box. The card gets routed in the postal system until it reaches its destination. Your parents need not be sitting there waiting for the card to arrive. UDP works much like the postal system.

In UDP, packets can be lost or delivered out of order. However, TCP expends extra effort to ensure not only that packets are delivered, but that they are delivered in the order in which they were sent. This extra work done by TCP makes it slower than UPD. The TCP connection works like a water pipe; both ends of this pipe are called *sockets*. Water flows from one socket to the other, as a stream. The pipe has a capacity, and in TCP, this is called the *buffer size*.

Both TCP and UDP have their own merits and are suitable for different applications. Since UDP is fast but unreliable, it is suitable for multimedia applications or voice over IP (VOIP) since in such applications, losing a small number of packets or re-ordering a few is tolerable. You only notice this with minor flickering in a movie clip or minor voice cutoffs. However, for applications such as Web banking, receiving every packet is essential even if this is going to make the application slower. TCP is more suitable for such applications. For instance, if you are paying a bill on-line, and the payee account number happened to be split into two packets, losing one of these packets would make it impossible to complete the transaction.

6.1.2   The World Wide Web

The World Wide Web is a collection of documents available through the Internet. These documents include images, multimedia files, and most importantly, Hyper Text Markup Language (HTML) files, in addition to server programs that generate HTML output. The WWW is not the Internet, and the Internet is not the WWW. The WWW is simply an application built on top of the Internet; email is another application built on the Internet. These applications rely on the services provided by the Internet, but they specify their own application-level protocols. When you communicate with your friends over the phone, you have to play by the rules set by the telephone system. On top of these protocols, you have your own (application-level) protocols. These rules could include not calling after midnight or before 10AM or not calling if you do not have enough remaining minutes on your cell phone. The protocol of WWW is called HTTP, which stands for Hyper Text Transfer Protocol. SMTP, IMAP, and POP3 are the protocols used by email. Figure 6.4 positions the Web and email within the Internet architecture.

So, when you requested the page `www.hrw.org`, the browser had to follow the five TCP steps outlined earlier to receive the HTML file. The missing link, though, is that the browser (the client) must request a connection with the Web server specifying an IP address and a port number. What is the IP address corresponding to `www.hrw.org`? To answer this question, we need to understand what a Universal Resource Locator (URL) is.

Universal Resource Locators

A *Universal Resource Locator* is a name given to a resource on the Web. The URL

    http://www.hrw.org/en/news

has several components. The **http://** prefix specifies which protocol is being used, HTTP, which is the protocol of the Web. **www.hrw.org** is the name of the server machine your client is trying to connect to. The last part, **/en/news**, is the name of a file or program stored on the server machine.

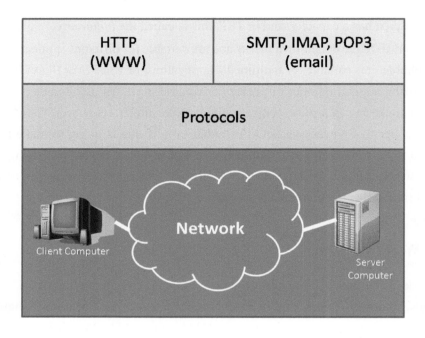

Figure 6.4: WWW and email are applications built on the Internet

Naming service

Fortunately, one does not need to remember the IP address of the `www.hrw.org` server. When someone requires a telephone number, they typically resort to the phone book to look it up. All they need to remember is the name of the party they would like to call. On the Web, `www.hrw.org` is the name of the server computer. Your browser uses the equivalent of the telephone book to translate this symbolic name to an IP address. There are special servers that implement such a "phone book" for the Web. These are called *naming servers* or *name servers*. The browser communicates with a nearby (local) naming server to look up the IP address for `www.hrw.org`. As shown in Figure 6.5, the client sends a *lookup* request to the naming server, specifying a symbolic name, and the naming server responds with the corresponding IP address.

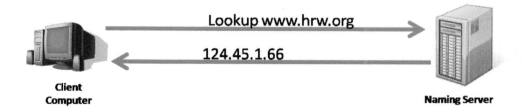

Figure 6.5: High-level view of the naming service

The implementation of the naming service is still more complicated than this simplistic explanation. Though it is feasible for every naming server to record the IP addresses of all the servers on the planet, this approach is not desirable because every time a new server is added to the Internet, all such naming servers must be updated. This is very costly, considering the number of existing naming servers and the rate of new servers being added to the Internet.

Names on the Internet are organized as a tree (Figure 6.6). Each vertex above the horizontal line has an associated naming server that only keeps information about its descendants. For instance, the `org` naming server keeps information about the `hrw` naming server, and `hrw` records the IP addresses of all the machines under (descendants of) `hrw`, including `www`. Leaves of this tree are documents or programs. A path from the root to a leaf corresponds to a symbolic name when read in reverse. Since in a tree there is a unique path from the root to every other vertex, the generated names are unique. For example, the machine `www` under `cbc` is different from that with the same name under `hrw`, and this is differentiated by writing the full name: `www.cbc.ca` or `www.hrw.org`.

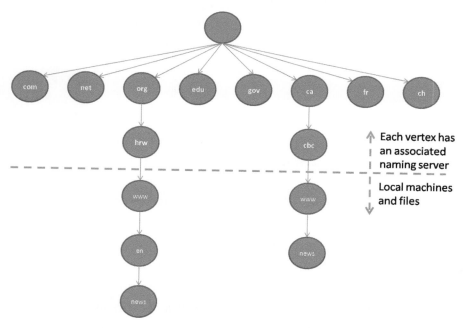

Figure 6.6: Tree organization of names

In such an organization, the local naming server communicates with other naming servers to resolve a name to an IP address. This is illustrated in Figure 6.7. When the local naming server receives a lookup request for `www.hrw.org` from the browser, it knows that it should contact the naming server that handles the `org` domain. Any address that ends with `org` must be registered with the `org` naming server. The `org` naming server examines the local naming server's request and provides it with the IP address for the naming server that handles `hrw.org`. The local naming server sends another request to the `hrw.org` naming server. `www` is typically the name of an actual computer registered with the `hrw.org` naming server. So, the latter supplies the IP address of the `www` machine to the local naming server, which passes it back to the browser. Now the browser has the IP address for `www.hrw.org`, and it can request a TCP connection with this server. The naming servers make use of TCP/IP to communicate with each other as well.

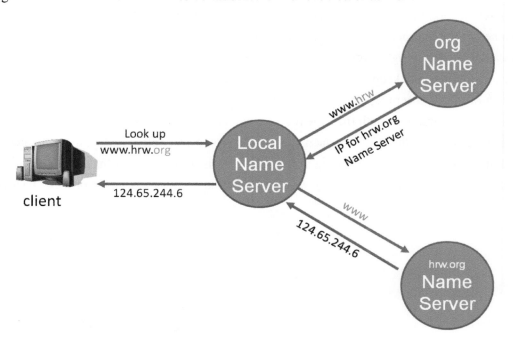

Figure 6.7: Illustration of name resolution

Note that in such an organization, the `hrw.org` naming server can add and remove server computers without having to update the `org` naming server. The latter must be updated only if a new Web site is added under the `org` domain.

To hide the latency incurred by the communication of the naming servers, the local naming server can *cache* the recently used names. That is, they keep a file, listing the recently visited Web sites and their corresponding IP addresses, so that if a client requests a look up of a name that is already in the cache, there will be no need to communicate with other servers. Unlike hardware caches, this cache is stored as a file on the hard disk of the local name server. The client itself can also cache names so that it saves itself from communicating with the local naming server unnecessarily.

Hyper Text Transfer Protocol

Now that the connection between the browser and the Web server is established, what kind of language do they speak with each other? They speak *HTTP*. That is, HTTP defines the structure (syntax) and meaning (semantics) of messages being exchanged between the browser and the Web server. For instance, the browser needs to be able to say: *get me the file index.html*. The server must

Example request:
```
GET /index.html HTTP/1.1
```

Example Response:
```
HTTP/1.1 200 OK
Date:  Sat, 15 Nov 2009 14:55:11 GMT
Server:  Apache/2.0.47
Accept-Ranges:  bytes
Content-Length:  1107
Connection:  close
Content-Type:  text/html; charset=ISO-8859-1
```

```
<HTML>
      <p>
           Welcome to our Website
      </p>
      <p>
           blah blah · · ·
      </p>
</HTML>
```

Figure 6.8: An example GET request with a sample server response

send a reply back. In what format does the server send the reply back?

In HTTP there are two types of messages. *Requests* are sent from the client to the server, and *responses* are sent back from the server to the client. The two major request messages are called GET and POST. The GET message is typically generated every time a hyperlink is clicked. The POST request is typically generated when you fill in form data and press a *submit* button, such as when you log into your email account. The general HTTP message structure is as follows:

Header
Empty line
Optional message

An example GET request and a sample response are given in Figure 6.8. The last part of the request HTTP/1.1 is specifying the protocol and the version (**1.1**). Note that the request must be followed by an empty line.

6.2 Secure Communication

When someone tries to log into their Internet banking application, a `POST` request that contains the login information is sent from the browser to the server hosting the banking application. What if someone manages to get this message and acquire your banking information? This is definitely possible if no extra measures are taken. First, we need to understand the kinds of threats that exist with communication so that we know how to counter them.

There are three major types of threats that may compromise communication:

1. **Interception:** This type of threat takes place when a party obtains unauthorized access to messages, data, or services. If someone gets your login information, this is interception. Another example is if someone breaks into the tax records and obtains your confidential tax information.

2. **Modification:** This type of threat takes place when an unauthorized change of messages, data, or services occurs. For instance, messages can be intercepted and changed before they arrive at their destination.

3. **Fabrication:** This type of threat refers to the unauthorized creation of messages, data, or services. A phishing email message, such as one pretending to be sent from your bank requesting that you update your information is an example of a fabrication threat.

Figure 6.9 shows a phishing message that I received. This message is asking me to verify my login information with the ICICI Bank. They want me to update this information by following the link `https:\\infinity.icicibank.co.in/loginrestore-session/server`. This is a fake link, and clicking on it will take me to `e-parts4u.com` instead. There is indeed an ICICI Bank, but the people who sent me this email have nothing to do with it. If someone falls into this phishing trap and submits his ICICI Bank login information, he will be sent to the site `e-parts4u.com` instead. The result would be that he accidentally gives his login information to a scam artist, who will likely misuse it. We will come back to this example, but first we must look at the general techniques employed on the Web to counter these threats.

To guard against these threats, two types of security measures can be taken.

1. **Encryption:** Encryption is encoding data and messages so that only the intended parties can decode them. For example, when you submit your credit card number to a trusted site, it must be sent in an encrypted way over the network. Internet scam artists could be listening to the channel, and if the message is not encrypted, your credit card number could end up in their hands.

2. **Authentication:** Authentication is verifying that the claimed identity by some party is authentic. The phishers who sent the message in Figure 6.9 are falsely claiming to be the ICICI Bank. We need an authentication mechanism that allows us verify whether a certain site or message belongs to the ICICI bank or the phishers.

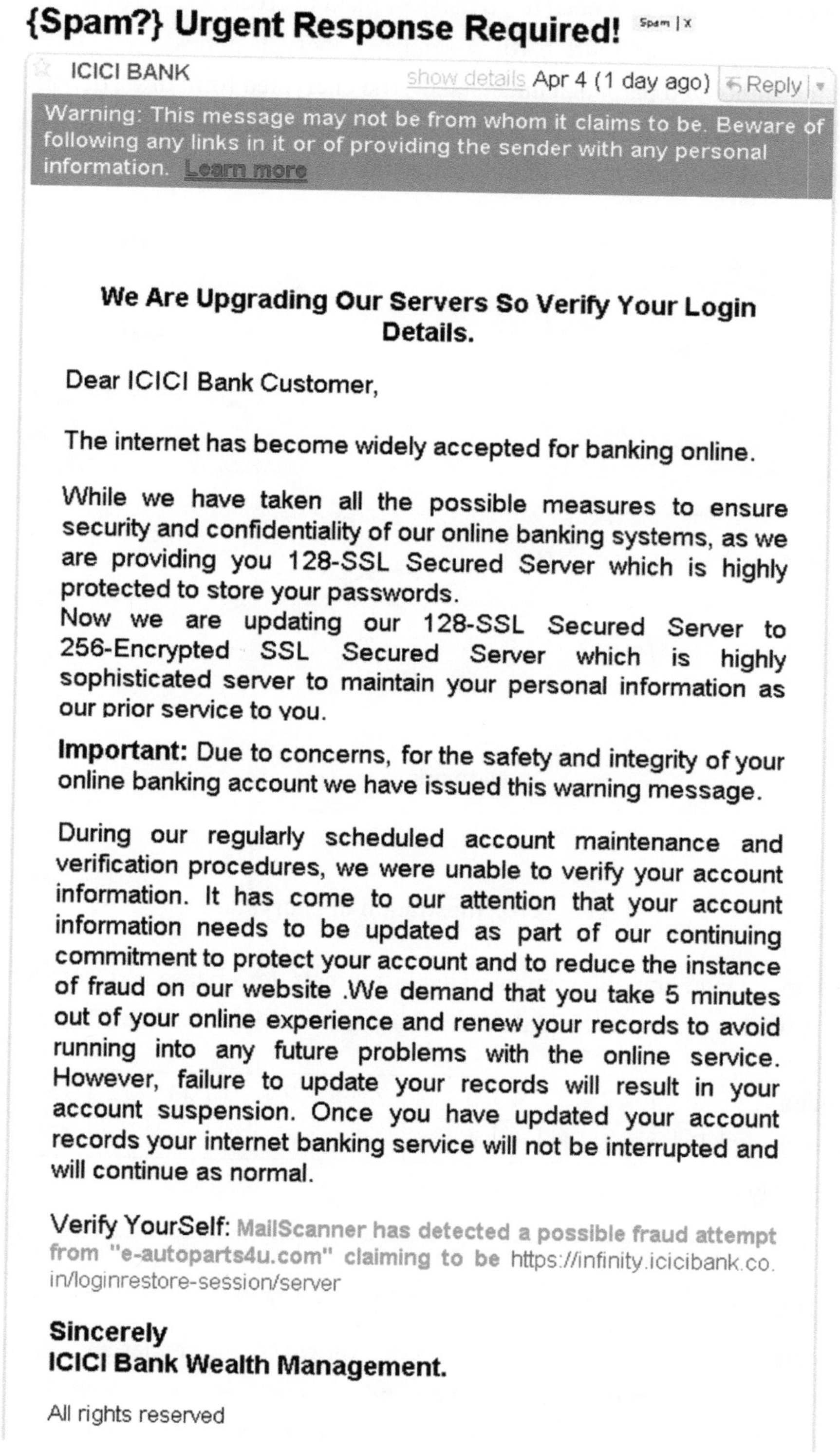

{Spam?} Urgent Response Required! _{Spam | x}

☆ ICICI BANK   show details Apr 4 (1 day ago) ↩ Reply ▾

Warning: This message may not be from whom it claims to be. Beware of
following any links in it or of providing the sender with any personal
information. Learn more

We Are Upgrading Our Servers So Verify Your Login Details.

Dear ICICI Bank Customer,

The internet has become widely accepted for banking online.

While we have taken all the possible measures to ensure
security and confidentiality of our online banking systems, as we
are providing you 128-SSL Secured Server which is highly
protected to store your passwords.
Now we are updating our 128-SSL Secured Server to
256-Encrypted SSL Secured Server which is highly
sophisticated server to maintain your personal information as
our prior service to you.

Important: Due to concerns, for the safety and integrity of your
online banking account we have issued this warning message.

During our regularly scheduled account maintenance and
verification procedures, we were unable to verify your account
information. It has come to our attention that your account
information needs to be updated as part of our continuing
commitment to protect your account and to reduce the instance
of fraud on our website .We demand that you take 5 minutes
out of your online experience and renew your records to avoid
running into any future problems with the online service.
However, failure to update your records will result in your
account suspension. Once you have updated your account
records your internet banking service will not be interrupted and
will continue as normal.

Verify YourSelf: MailScanner has detected a possible fraud attempt
from "e-autoparts4u.com" claiming to be https://infinity.icicibank.co.
in/loginrestore-session/server

Sincerely
ICICI Bank Wealth Management.

All rights reserved

Figure 6.9: A phishing email message

Encryption and authentication need to go hand-in-hand to create secure channels.

Encryption is illustrated in Figure 6.10. A sender S encrypts a message P into a form that no one other than the authorized party can understand. The encrypted form of P, denoted by C, is sent over the network. When the intended receiver R receives C, R will be able to decrypt C, turning it back to P. P is called the *plain-text*, and C is called the *cipher-text*.

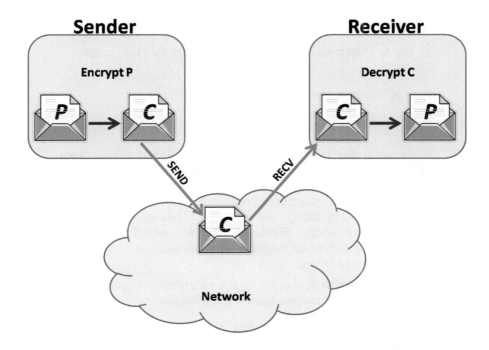

Figure 6.10: Illustration of encryption

Before we understand how this can guard against threats, let's pause and learn a bit more about how encryption works. Consider the plain-text: *Peeking into CS*, which is a 15-character message:

index	0	1	2	3	4	5	6	7	8	9	10	11	12	13	14
character	P	e	e	k	i	n	g		i	n	t	o		C	S

One simple way to encrypt this message is to use a permutation key:

0	1	2	3	4	5	6	7	8	9	10	11	12	13	14
13	0	4	3	14	10	1	8	12	11	6	7	2	5	9

This key must be kept secret and should be only known by the sender and receiver. They key tells the sender how to encrypt the message, and it tells the receiver how to decrypt it. It simply tells the sender to shuffle the message in a certain way. Character 0 in the plain-text goes to index 13 in the cipher-text, character 1 of the plain-text goes to index 0 in the cipher-text, and so on, generating the cipher-text *eg keCto SnniPi*:

index	0	1	2	3	4	5	6	7	8	9	10	11	12	13	14
character	e	g		k	e	C	t	o		S	n	n	i	P	i

Since the receiver knows the secret key, the receiver can easily reverse this process and construct the plain-text back from the cipher-text.

While actual *cryptosystems* use similar ideas, this approach does not define a good encryption algorithm. An intruder could spend enough time on some intercepted messages to infer the secret key. Once the secret key is compromised, communication is no longer confidential.

Example 6.2

> Say an intruder intercepts the cipher-text: *amd*. If the intruder knows that a permutation key is employed for encryption, she can tell that one of the following possibilities must be the plain text: adm, mad, mda, dam, and dma. Since only mad and dam make sense, she can limit the possibilities for the permutation key to two. Given more cipher-text messages and a little bit more effort, the intruder will be able to infer the secret key. This is an example with a very small message (3 characters), and there are only 3! = 6 possibilities for arranging 3 characters, including the cipher-text itself. Nevertheless, if the message is larger, the number of possibilities becomes astronomical. For instance, if the message is 20 characters long, there are 20! = 2,432,902,008,176,640,000 possibilities. This makes cracking the key much harder, but not necessarily impossible. Given enough resources and time, the secret key can be eventually cracked.

There are two big differences between our simple example and real systems. First, real-life encryption algorithms are far more complicated, making it impossible for an intruder to infer the key. Second, encryption is done at the bit-level, rather than the character-level. This makes the message larger and the number of possibilities much larger, making it harder to crack a key. However, our example should serve the purpose of giving us an idea of how cryptosystems work.

Cryptosystems guard against the three types of threats listed earlier. Let P, C, and $K_{S,R}$ respectively be the plain-text, the cipher-text, and the shared, secret key between S and R. The function ENCRYPT$(P, K_{S,R})$ encrypts P using $K_{S,R}$, generating the cipher-text C, or $C \leftarrow$ ENCRYPT$(P, K_{S,R})$. Similarly, DECRYPT$(C, K_{S,R})$ decrypts C using $K_{S,R}$, generating the plain-text P, or $P \leftarrow$ DECRYPT$(C, K_{S,R})$.

Since the intruder does not know the secret key $K_{S,R}$, she will not be able to decrypt C and therefore cannot recover the message P. To modify an intercepted cipher-text C, the intruder needs the secret key to recover P from C ($P \leftarrow$ DECRYPT$(C, K_{S,R})$), change P to $\hat{P}$, encrypt it to $\hat{C}$ ($\hat{C} \leftarrow$ ENCRYPT$(\hat{P}, K_{S,R})$), and send $\hat{C}$. Otherwise, if the intruder does not know the secret key, any other changes will simply corrupt the message C to become D. When the receiver decrypts D, he will discover that it is a corrupted message and simply drop it. A similar argument applies to fabrication.

6.2.1　Types of cryptosystems

There are two kinds of Encryption systems. In the *symmetric* type, the communicating parties share a secret key, which is used for encryption and decryption. These are also called *secret* or *shared-key* cryptosystems. The simple permutation example that we discussed earlier falls in this category.

The second type is the *asymmetric* or *public-key* cryptosystems. These make use of a pair of keys for each communicating party: a *private-key*, which is always kept secret and is never shared with anyone, and a *public-key* which is made available publicly. These keys are generated in such a way that they are reciprocal, yet it is not easy to construct a private-key given the public one. Reciprocity means that if a message is encrypted using the public key, it can be decrypted only using the matching private key and vice versa.

Example 6.3

> Consider a combination lock where a unique code unlocks it. Say that I construct several identical copies of this same lock, and each one can be unlocked only with the secret code, which I keep to myself. In this analogy, the lock is the public-key, and the secret code is the private-key. I distribute these locks to all my friends, so that if one of them wants to send me a confidential document, he or she puts the document into a metal box and lock it with the combination lock that I provided. If someone intercepts the box, they will not be able to look inside and see its contents, unless they know the secret code. Since no one knows this secret code except me, the document will remain confidential.

If X is a communicating party, K_X^+ denotes X's public-key, and K_X^- denotes X's private-key. To achieve encryption of plain-text P in an asymmetric system, the sender S makes use of the receiver's R public-key to encrypt the message. That is, S sends the cipher-text C, such that $C \leftarrow$ ENCRYPT(P, K_R^+). C has the property that only R's private-key can recover P from C, or $P \leftarrow$ DECRYPT(C, K_R^-). Only R knows K_R^-, and in this way, R sent S a confidential message.

However, encryption alone is insufficient to guarantee secure communication. If messages are being encrypted to guard against intruders, we also need to make sure that the identity of the person with whom we are communicating is confirmed. *Authentication* is as important as encryption.

Authentication can be achieved using *digital signatures*. In an asymmetric cryptosystem, S's digital signature can be ENCRYPT(S, K_S^-), where $ds \leftarrow$ ENCRYPT(S, K_S^-). That is, S can encrypt its identity, S, using its private key K_S^-. Then S composes the plain-text $[S, ds]$, and encrypts it using R's public-key ENCRYPT$([S, ds], K_R^+)$, with $C \leftarrow$ ENCRYPT$([S, ds], K_R^+)$. The message $[S, ds]$ has two components, S's identity and S's digital signature, ds.

C is confidential and can be opened only by R. When R recovers $[S, ds]$, the first part of this message is telling R that this message is from S, or at least this is what is claimed. How does R

know for sure that this message is from S? After all, anyone can put S into a message and encrypt it with R's public-key, which is known to everybody. R authenticates S using the second part of the message, the digital signature ds. ds is an encrypted message using S's private-key. R can recover the original message by applying S's public-key, which is known to everyone. If $S \leftarrow$ ENCRYPT(ds, K_S^+), then R authenticates S. That is, S is whom it claims to be: only S knows S's private-key K_S^-, so no one else could have generated this particular ds.

6.2.2 Digital certificates

A *digital certificate* is a special kind of a message that a server S sends to a browser (client) B, and it allows B to authenticate S's identity. Digital certificates are provided for a fee through dedicated trusted organizations, called *certification authorities* (CA). A digital certificate that belongs to a server S includes:

- S's public-key, K_S^+

- S's identity (the host name part of the URL)

- an expiration date for the digital certificate

- the name of the CA offering the digital certificate

- a serial number

- a digital signature ds generated by encrypting S's identity using CA's private-key. That is, $ds \leftarrow$ ENCRYPT(S, K_{CA}^-).

Figure 6.11 shows an example of a digital certificate viewed with the Firefox browser. This certificate is issued to `easyweb.tdcanadatrust.com`; that is S, the server's identity, is `easyweb.tdcanadatrust.com`. The server's public-key can be found under the details tab, which is given using the hexadecimal number system.

Secure Socket Layer

HTTP with security (HTTPS) enhances the HTTP protocol to make communication secure. It makes use of a security protocol called the *Secure Socket Layer* (SSL). SSL uses a combination of symmetric and asymmetric key cryptosystems to establish secure channels and to allow browsers to authenticate servers. SSL is illustrated in Figure 6.12.

SSL is automatically turned on when the protocol in the URL is `https` instead of `http` (such as the examples in Figure 6.13). The browser B requests a secure connection with the server S. S replies by sending its digital certificate to B. B decrypts the digital signature ds included in the certificate, using K_{CA}^+, which is publicly known. If decoding ds yields S, B authenticates S. B also checks for other indications, such as making sure the certificate is not expired. If the certificate is valid, the browser shows a lock symbol (see the examples in Figure 6.13). If, however, there is

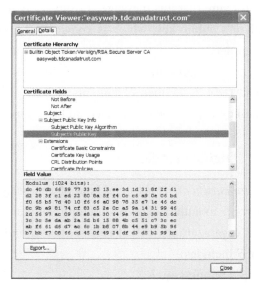

Figure 6.11: Viewing a digital certificate with Firefox

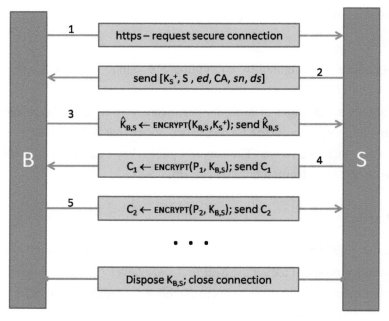

Message 2 – ed: expiry date of the certificate; sn: serial number;

ds : digital signature such that $ds \leftarrow \text{ENCRYPT}(S, K_{CA}^-)$

Message 3 – $\hat{K}_{B,S}$ is the encryption of $K_{B,S}$, that is $\hat{K}_{B,S} \leftarrow \text{ENCRYPT}(K_{B,S}, K_S^+)$

Message 4 – any plain-text P sent and received is encrypted using $K_{B,S}$

Figure 6.12: Illustrating the Secure Socket Layer

something wrong with the certificate, the lock symbol either disappears (Internet Explorer) or it is shown with a warning (Firefox) as Figure 6.14 depicts.

If the certificate is valid, B generates a secret shared-key $K_{B,S}$ and sends to S. However, this key must remain a secret between B and S. So, B uses S's public-key to encrypt $K_{B,S}$, generating the cipher-text: ENCRYPT($K_{B,S}, K_S^+$). Now $K_{B,S}$ can be used to encrypt the communication between R and S during this session. The key will then be disposed off. Each time B requires a secure connection with S, a new disposable secret-key is generated and used for one session only.

Returning to the phishing example, the phishers wanted to fool me into making me believe I am submitting my information to

`https:\\infinity.icicibank.co.in/loginrestore-session/server`.

The `icicibank` part of the URL makes it look like the URL belongs to the ICICI Bank, and the `https` makes it look like the connection will be secure. However, typing this address into the browser's URL field generates a browser warning. In Figure 6.14(a), the lock symbol disappeared (in Internet Explorer), and in Figure 6.14(b), the lock is shown with a warning symbol (in FireFox). Both are indications that the browser detected an invalid or a non-existent digital certificate.

(a)

(b)

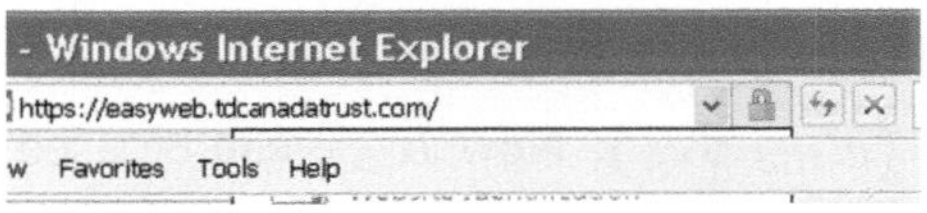

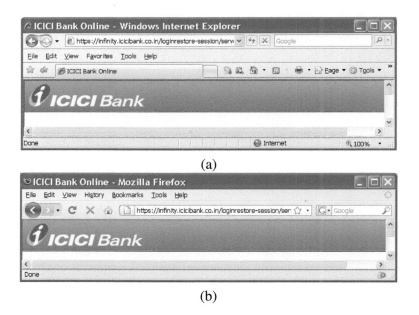

Figure 6.13: Lock symbol indicating a valid certificate in (a) Internet Explorer and (b) Firefox

(a)

(b)

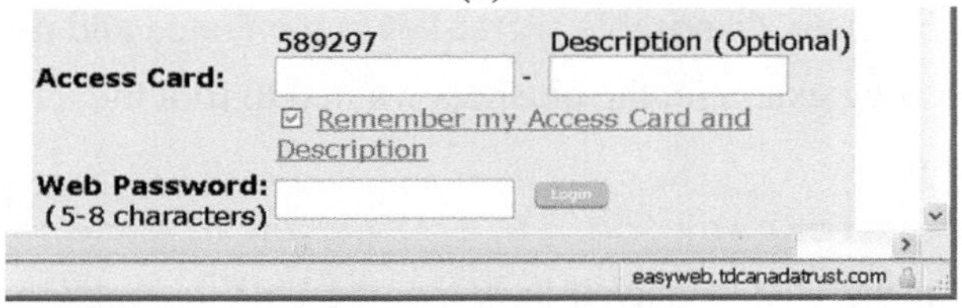

Figure 6.14: Indication of an invalid certificate in (a) Internet Explorer and(b) Firefox

Exercises

1. Which of the following is a legal IP address?

   (a) 1.2.3.-1

   (b) 1.2.3.4

   (c) 1000.2000.3.4

2. What are the differences and similarities between TCP and UDP?

3. If a packet is lost, how do you think TCP tries to recover it?

4. What are the advantages of organizing names as a tree in the Internet?

5. In the early days of the Internet, what used to be called ARPANET, naming was implemented as a flat file. That is, the names and their corresponding IP addresses were organized in the same way the white pages are organized. Why was this an acceptable design then, and why it is no longer acceptable?

6. How would it be possible for a local name server to translate the name www.facebook.com without talking to any other naming server (.com or facebook.com)?

7. Which HTTP request is likely generated when a hyperlink is clicked?

8. Which HTTP request is likely generated when a form submit button is clicked?

9. Research the HEAD HTTP request, and explain what it does.

10. What happens if the required empty line in an HTTP request is mistakenly omitted?

11. How many possibilities are there to encrypt the plain-text *Peeking into CS* using our simple permutation key approach? If we replace each character in the plain-text with its 8-bit ASCII code, and then applied the permutation key, how many possibilities would there be for corresponding cipher-texts?

12. Using the permutation key described in this chapter, determine the plain-text from the following cipher-text: *oQoguntiu? seTh*.

13. What are the advantages of asymmetric-key cryptosystems over symmetric-key cryptosystems?

14. Using the combination lock analogy discussed in this chapter, describe a protocol that allows your friends to authenticate you.

15. Why does not the server authenticate the browser with SSL?

16. Electronic contract signing requires a unique association between the contract itself and the identity of the signer. Develop an appropriate digital signature for contract-signing using asymmetric cryptography.

Answers to Selected Exercises

Chapter 1

1. Input: a deck of 52 cards; output: the 52 cards sorted as follows: 12 heart cards, 12 diamond cards, 12 club cards, and 12 spade cards; each 12 cards is sorted from 1 (Ace) to 10, followed by Jack, Queen, and King.

4. **Algorithm** — *Find(pile of papers, X)* _____
   Input: Pile of exam papers, student id x
   Output: exam paper for student x
   $i = 1$
   Repeat the following steps
   If the exam paper at position 1 has the id x, retrieve this paper; stop
   ___ *Else increment i by 1* _____

7. $50\% \times$ CLASS_SIZE + $50\% \times$ INSTRUCTOR_RATINGS is not an appropriate objective value. This formula favors higher instructor ratings, but it also favors larger classes. A better formula would be: $50\% \times$ INSTRUCTOR_RATINGS - $50\% \times$ CLASS_SIZE.

10. Since this robot does not turn right, this must be accomplished through making three consecutive left turns. Hence, the only change in the algorithm is that each single right turn is replaced by three consecutive left turns.

11. A music CD is an example of random access memory because you can jump from one track to another without having to go through the other tracks.

15. (a) $2000 \times 8 = 16000$ bits. (b) There are 6 distinct characters, so we need at least 3 bits per character since $2^3 = 8 > 6$ but $2^2 = 4 < 6$.

Chapter 2

2. (a) True. (b) This is false only when you pass the course but do not get an A; otherwise, it is true. (c) Since not all citizens vote in elections, this can be also true or false. (d) True.

3. (a) $\forall x(M(x) \rightarrow O(x))$. (b) $\exists x(W(x) \wedge O(x))$. (c) $\forall x(M(x) \rightarrow (F(x) \vee Z(x)))$.

5. These are equivalent when $\forall x P(x)$ is true.

6. (a)

A	B	$A \cap B$	$A \cup (A \cap B)$
F	F	F	F
F	T	F	F
T	F	F	T
T	T	T	T

8. (a) This is not a function since a person can visit many countries. (b) This not a function: a person can be a citizen of more than one country. (c) This is a function because a person is born in one and only one place.

11. **Algorithm** — *equal(A, B)* ——————————————————————

Input: two sets A and B

Output: true if $A = B$, false otherwise

For each element $x \in A$

if $x \notin B$ then return false

For each element $x \in B$

if $x \notin A$ then return false

return true
——

12. **Algorithm** — *union(A, B)* ——————————————————————

Input: two sets A and B

Output: $A \cup B$

Let C be an initially empty set

For each element $x \in A$

Add x to C

For each element $x \in B$

if $x \notin A$ then Add x to C

return C
——

13. **Algorithm** — *intersection(A, B)* ——————————————————

Input: two sets A and B

Output: $A \cap B$

Let C be an initially empty set

For each element $x \in A$

if $x \in B$ then add x to C

return C
——

202

Chapter 3

1. **Algorithm** — *intersection(M)* _____

   Input: *adjacency n × m matrix M*

   Output: *true if M is symmetric, false otherwise*

   For each i from 0 to n − 1, in order

      For each j from 0 to m − 1, in order

         If $M[i][j] \neq M[j][i]$ then return false

   ____*return true*_____

4. The circuit is the empty list.

6. Any graph of $n > 1$ vertices where each vertex is adjacent to every other vertex requires n colors. Such a graph is called a *full* graph.

9. **Algorithm** — *numOfVertices(T)* _____

   Input: *binary tree T*

   Output: *number of vertices in T*

   Let r be the root vertex of T

   Let toExplore be a list of vertices initially containing r only; that is, toExplore = [r]

   counter = 0

   Repeat the following until toExplore becomes empty

      Replace the first vertex of toExplore with its children, if any

      (if the vertex is a leaf, simply delete it)

   ____*Increment counter*_____

12. 4 bits are needed since $2^4 = 16 > 10$ and $2^3 = 8 < 10$.

13. $4 \times 10000 = 40000$.

16. States: CLOSED, OPEN, OPENNING (in motion), and CLOSING (in motion). Events: REMOTE (remote button is pressed), SENSOR (sensor senses an object), ALLWUP (the door is all the way up), TCHFLR (the door touches the floor)

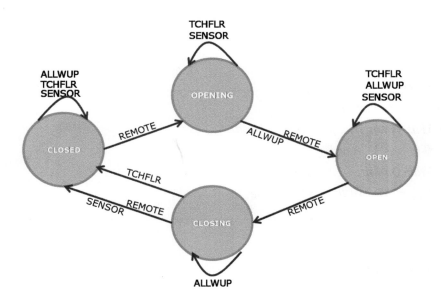

Chapter 4

5. Since the "participants" in PLAY "are" TEAM, A new schema PLAYS will be created with the primary keys of the participants as columns. Hence, PLAYS will have the columns TEAM_ID1 and TEAM_ID2 in addition to PLAYS attributes.

7. (a)

```
SELECT   *
FROM     PROJECT
WHERE    Salary > 30000 ;
```

(c)

```
SELECT   *
FROM     PROJECT
WHERE    Salary > 30000
OR       City ! = 'Toronto' ;
```

(e)

```
SELECT   *
FROM     PROJECT, DEPARTMENT, EMPLOYEE
WHERE    PROJECT.Dnumber = DEPARTMENT.Dnumber
AND      DEPARTMENT.MGR_SIN = EMPLOYEE.IS
AND      EMPLOYEE.Gender = 'Female' ;
```

(g)

```
SELECT      Pnumber, SUM(Hours)
FROM        PROJECT
GROUP BY    Pnumber ;
```

(i)

```
SELECT    *
FROM      EMPLOYEE
WHERE     NOT EXISTS (
                    SELECT    *
                    FROM      PROJECT, DEPARTMENT, WORKS_ON
                    WHERE     PROJECT.Dnumber = DEPARTMENT.Dnumber
                    AND       WORKS_ON.Pnumber = EMPLOYEE.Pnumber
                    AND       WORKS_ON.SIN = EMPLOYEE.SIN
                              AND Dname = 'IT'
                    ) ;
```

9. **SINGER**

ID	Name	Bio	Website

ALBUM

ID	Title	ReleaseDate

SONG

ID	Title	ReleaseDate

PERFORMS

Song_ID	Singer_ID

CONTAINS

Song_ID	Album_ID

(a)

```
SELECT    Title, Duration, Genre
FROM      SONG, SINGER, PERFORMS
WHERE     SONG.ID = PERFORMS.Song_ID
AND       SINGER.ID = PERFORMS.Singer_ID
AND       SINGER.Name = 'Michael Jackson' ;
```

205

(b)

```
SELECT    ALBUM.Title, ReleaseDate
FROM      SONG, SINGER, PERFORMS
WHERE     SONG.ID = PERFORMS.Song_ID
AND       SINGER.ID = PERFORMS.Singer_ID
AND       ( SINGER.Name = 'Michael Jackson'
OR        SINGER.Name = 'Jennifer Lopez' ) ;
```

Chapter 6

1. (a) is invalid because -1 is not between 0 and 255. (b) is valid. (c) is not.

3. Ensuring packet delivery is accomplished through an acknowledgment mechanism. When A sends a packet to B, A waits for an acknowledgment from B that the packet was successfully delivered. If A does not receive an acknowledgment, A assumes that the packet was lost and re-sends it. A keeps on sending a packet until it is acknowledged. Note that if A does not receive an acknowledgment, this does not necessarily mean that the original packet was lost since it could be the case that the acknowledgment itself was lost. However, A does not have a mechanism differentiate, so it always assumes that the original packet was lost.

5. A flat file naming structure was acceptable because (1) the number of computers on the network was low, and (2) this allowed the naming service to be centrally managed. Today, the size of the Internet is huge, in terms of the number of computers, and central management of such a vast network is infeasible.

6. This can be accomplished through a technique called *caching*. When the local name server resolves www.facebook.com, it keeps a record of it on the form of (URL, IP) pair. This allows future lookup requests to be satisfied by the local name server without the need to talk to other name servers. The cache entries will be discarded if they are not used for a long time.

10. A "bad request" error message is generated by the Web server.

11. There are 15 characters in the message *Peeking into CS*; hence, there are 15! = 1,307,674,368,000 possibilities to re-arrange these characters in the cipher-text. If each character is replaced by its ASCII 8-bit representation, the number of possibilities becomes $8 \times 15! = 10,461,394,944,000$.

14. Since I am the only one who knows the combination for the lock, my friend sends me a challenge word in a box locked by my lock. I am the only one who can unlock the box and

recover the challenge word. In future communication, I can use this challenge word as a proof of my identity. Yet, I have to use it in a secure way; otherwise, it can be compromised.

207

Credits & Acknowledgments

The spreadsheet design discussion is due to Mishtu Banerjee. The robot example is based on Seymour Papert's turtle Geometry [4] and the associated children's programming language, Logo.

Our propositional logic discussion is influenced by the thorough treatment of Rosen [5].

The Konigsberg bridges example and the Euler circuit algorithm are based on the treatment of Rosen [5]. The traffic example and its corresponding colored graph is a simplified version of the one introduced by Aho *et al.* [1]. Dijkstra's single-source shortest path is also influenced by Aho *et al.* [1]. Huffman's coding algorithm is adapted from the one presented by Rosen [5]. Our door controllers finite state machines are extensions of a similar and simpler example by Sipser [6].

The example of the simple company in Chapter 4 is a simplified version of that of Elmasri and Navathe [3]. The design part of the chapter is largely based on their work. The forestry ERD example is a simplified version of the one presented by Bradley [2].

I am thankful to the students and instructors at the University of Calgary who have used an earlier edition of this work. In particular, my thanks go to Adelaine Hansson, Trent Cherak, and Laura Williams who uncovered a few errors.

[1] A. V. Aho, J. D. Ullman, and J. E. Hopcroft. *Data Structures and Algorithms*. Addison Wesley, 1983.

[2] J. Bradley. *File and Data Base Techniques*. Holt, Rinehart, and Winston, 1982.

[3] R. Elmasri and S. B. Navathe. *Fundamentals of Database Systems, 5/e*. Addison Wesley, 2006.

[4] S. Papert. *The Children's Machine: Rethinking School in the Age of the Computer*. Basic Books, 1994.

[5] K. H. Rosen. *Discrete Mathematics and Its Applications, 6/e*. McGraw-Hill, 2007.

[6] M. Sipser. *Introduction to the Theory of Computation, 2/e*. Course Technology, 2005.

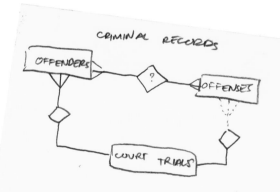